Published by Artisan Ideas, 2021.
By Ulf Avander
Layout and cover design: Andrea James Blaho
Technical Editor: Gerald Franklin (Norman, Oklahoma)

ISBN 9781733325035
Library of Congress Control Number: 2021934536
Printed in China.
Artisan Ideas is an imprint of **Artisan North America, Inc.**
Tel: 800-843-9567
Info@ArtisanIdeas.com

For a selection of reference books for knifemakers and blacksmiths visit our website: www.ArtisanIdeas.com.

Artisan North America
753 Valley Road
Watchung, NJ 07069-6120

Ordering information:
Quantity sales: Special discounts are available on quantity purchases by corporations, associations, and others. For details, contact the publisher at the address above. For single copies, please try your bookstore or knifemaking or blacksmithing supply store first. If unavailable this book can be ordered through: www.ArtisanIdeas.com.

To see our complete selection of books and DVDs on this and other subjects visit our website: **www.ArtisanIdeas.com**.

Authors!

If you have an idea for a book please contact us at: Info@ArtisanIdeas.com.
We'll be glad to hear from you and discuss your idea.

www.ArtisanIdeas.com.

Table of Contents

Antler Knife

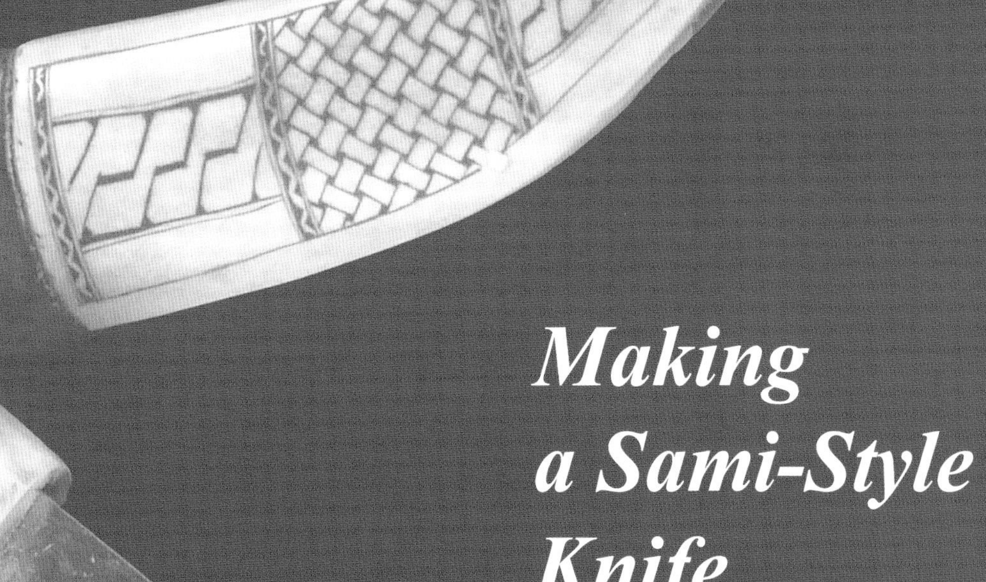

Making a Sami-Style Knife

The Sami-Style Knife Handle and Sheath: What You Need to Know Before Beginning

The author assumes you already have some knifemaking experience and that you will either make or acquire a knife blade for this project conforming to the type and dimensions given in the section "The Blade". Making the blade itself is not discussed.

The instructions in this book concern collecting and preparing the material for the handle and sheath (e.g. the antler, the leather, the wood and the bark), then using the material to build your Antler Knife and sheath the Sami way.

It is suggested that you read the book completely before beginning this project so that you can decide beforehand what material you will look for and prepare yourself and what material you might find easier to purchase.

Traditional knives and their sheaths used in northern Sweden, and in Lapland in general, employ the use of reindeer antler. As seen in the photo on this book's cover, the unique sheath for the traditional Sami-style* knife which Ulf Avander will teach you to construct consists of two sections: the bottom part made of reindeer antler and the top part, of leather. The knife's handle is made of hardwood and antler. The pommel and the guard are also made of antler.

As Ulf mentions later in this book, handles made solely of antler are very slippery and are also very cold. As attractive as it is, the knife you will construct is a functional Sami-style working knife for daily use and not an art knife, so it is essential that the handle is made to give you a good grip and does not employ too much antler in its construction.

Various spacers of Vulcan fiber, or birch bark if you prefer, will be used in the handle's construction and also some tin for use as a decorative band.

**The Sami (or Sapmi in the Sami language) are the nomadic people of Lapland, which includes parts of northern Norway, Sweden, Finland and Russia. At one time, in the English language, the Sami were referred to as Lapps or Laplanders, but these terms are now considered derogatory and are no longer used.*

The Antler Knife

Part I: Primary Materials and Preliminary Procedures

The Antler

In my experience, reindeer antler is preferable to moose antler. It has a more attractive finish after being worked on and polished. It also has a more beautiful color structure. Reindeer antler isn't normally as hard as moose antler and is therefore easier to work with.

In the Northern Sami language the uncastrated reindeer bull is usually called a *sarv* and a castrated reindeer a *härk*. The *sarv*'s antler is preferred, since it is normally of higher quality, both in density and in shape. The reindeer cow is called a *vaja*. Her antler is smaller and is not suitable for making a normal-sized knife.

To differentiate between an antler from a castrated and a un-castrated reindeer is not easy. With a shed antler, the form of the pedicle, which is the antler's connection to the skull, can be of some guidance. The antler from a bull should have a convex surface where it has detached from the skull, on the underside of the pedicle, while for the castrated bull, that surface is normally concave.

Antler with a flat cross section is usually better than antler with a round cross section, since a flat antler normally has less marrow which makes it easier to shape. Antler marrow is a porous, spongy, and softer material in comparison to the outer layers of the antler. Marrow will not take a polish, wears poorly, and discolors easily.

A shed antler is better to use than an antler from a butchered reindeer since the shed antler is fully-grown and normally has less color – which is a good thing, as we shall see. A shed antler can't normally be used if it has been lying outside on wet ground for more than two years. After that it starts to crack and it becomes mildewed and discolored. Sometimes however, if the antler is discolored to a moss green color it can still be of good quality inside.

Bleaching the Antler

A fresh antler is always more distinct in color then an old antler. Sun, rain, snow and age bleach the antler. If there is a need for extra bleaching the antler can be placed in cold running water (i.e. a stream or river) for at least one year. The blood will then be drawn from the antler. When it's time to dry an antler that has been in water for a long time it should be done outside since it gives off an unpleasant smell.

To bleach antler with chemicals such as hydrogen peroxide takes away the natural oils from the antler. This makes it harder to obtain a beautiful surface without additional artificial treatment. Chemical bleaching gives an unnatural, almost "dead" look, to the material.

Still, when the antler is too distinct in its coloration and you want to bleach it, the antler should be slightly sanded before beginning.

SAFETY WARNING: Read safety information about hydrogen peroxide before handling it! It will corrode your skin. It is also a highly reactive chemical. It reacts with, among other things, aluminum and copper.

Wrap some paper towels around the parts that are to be bleached and add a 35% solution (or as strong as you can make it) of hydrogen peroxide. Check periodically to make sure you do not over-bleach. When done, wash the antler thoroughly with water. Remember to use rubber gloves when handling hydrogen peroxide otherwise it will bleach your fingers and corrode your skin. You can also pour some hydrogen peroxide in a container (pay attention to what the container is made of) and let the pieces soak in the liquid. Don't re-use the hydrogen peroxide in which you soaked the antler and don't pour the used solution back with the unused portion.

Antler for the Handle

Because marrow is not as hard as the rest of the antler, the pieces you use for your knife handle should have as little marrow as possible. If there is too much, there is the risk that when finishing the handle you could easily sand it right down to the marrow.

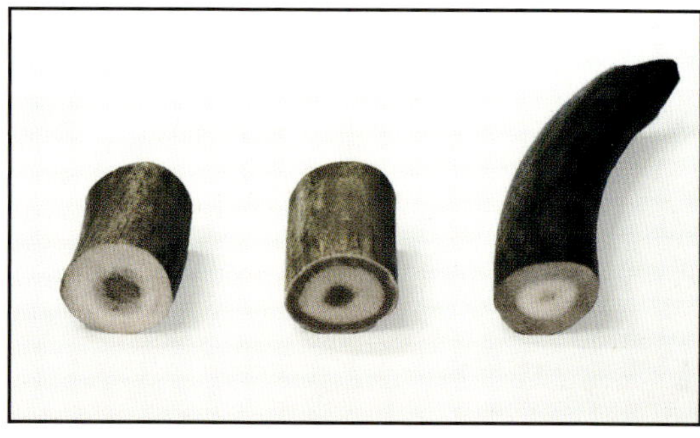

1 – The antler to the left in the photo has too much marrow to be useful. The middle piece is acceptable and the one to the right is perfect regarding the amount of marrow.

Every antler will contain some marrow, but the antler utilized for the handle must be compact and dense—so dense that a knifepoint can hardly be forced into the marrow.

A piece of antler that is roughly the same shape as the intended final shape and size of the knife handle, which is normally oval, is of course the most suitable because there is less chance that you will inadvertently sand or file the antler down to the marrow. Exposed marrow on the handle will gradually get darker and easily become dirty. There's also the risk that antler with too much marrow, after a period of use, will loosen from the tang. Marrow is very soft and won't withstand heavy use of your knife.

Antler for the Pommel

The section of antler to be used for the pommel is best taken from as close as possible to the antler crown since there is the least amount of marrow in that part. Generally, the amount of marrow increases in relation to the distance from the antler crown. Furthermore, the material close to the antler crown is the closest in shape to the desired "flared" shape of the pommel (see cover photo).

There are two major styles in the Sami design of an Antler Knife; the Southern Sami and the Northern Sami traditions. They differ both in form and patterning. The Southern Sami design is more geometric whereas the Northern style uses a softer, usually floral, motif. My procedure follows the Northern Sami style.

It is not necessary to use a piece of antler from close to the crown for the Southern Sami style because their pommel is not flared.

Antler for the Sheath

The section of antler to be used for the sheath (which has both an antler part and a leather part) should be taken either from the antler's main beam to achieve a straighter sheath, or from the frontal tine's hook if an angled sheath shape is desired.

NOTE: All antler used in making a Sami-style knife handle and sheath is sanded down smooth and shiny. The antler in this renowned, classic knife is not left rough or grooved.

The antler shouldn't be too curved along its length, nor should the front tine be too twisted, otherwise the sheath will either be too narrow or too thin. This becomes apparent when the two halves of the sheath are hollowed out when removing the marrow.

The piece of antler used for the sheath should not be too round either. This is because the marrow core is normally the same shape as the outer part of the antler (i.e., round, oval, or flat), and must be removed. The walls of the sheath may not be thick enough after the marrow is removed.

The ideal antler for an angled sheath is fairly flat and straight and is at about a 75-degree angle to the front tine. It should also be a heavy, shed antler.

A good weight for a high-quality shed antler is 3 lbs. to 4-1/2 lbs. (1.5 to 2-kgs).

The Wood

Curly-Grained Wood for the Handle

The curly-grained wood that I use for my Antler Knife handles comes from the roots of willow or birch. This is different than curly-grained birch which is well structured throughout the whole trunk and is commonly used for furniture.

The curly-grained wood I am referring to can also be found on the trunks of willow or birch trees as burls, but these are harder to find. It is also possible to use normal protuberances, but this wood is not as compact as the wood in a burl and does not have the noticeable and beautiful variation in grain structure that burl wood has.

With experience, trees with curly-grained wood in their roots can be recognized by their leaves and their visible roots.

2 – Root protuberance from a willow.

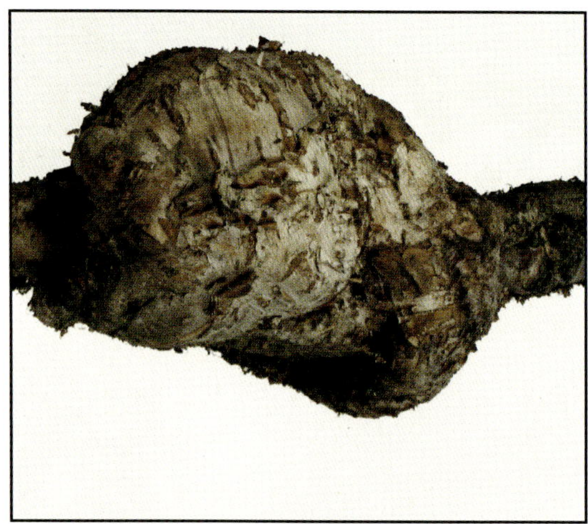

3 – An ordinary protuberance with a rough surface can give a nice texture to the handle.

The leaves are smaller and more numerous than those found on most other trees. These smaller leaves grow both on the tree's branches and also from small shoots growing out of the trunk. Some roots are often visible growing above the ground. They commonly have tiny shoots or suckers growing from them.

If the moss on the root is removed and you find a rough knot, cut away some of the bark. If you see the typical dots or "birds' eyes", you have found curly-grained wood.

Before you begin digging out the root, you should check on the condition of the tree's branches. The more dried-out dead branches you see, the likelier it is that there will be rot or decay in the roots. It is rare to find curly-grained wood without some rot.

When you have found curly-grained wood that you are satisfied with and you have obtained permission to cut it, the laborious work begins. You need to dig up and cut off the roots. Keep the main roots connected to the trunk or stump until you have cut off most of their length. By doing this the trunk can then be used as a lever.

Curly-grained willow wood is darker than birch. This difference becomes even more noticeable when oil is applied to it. Birch is harder and denser than willow. Normally willow roots become darker the closer they are to the heartwood. The most common curly-grained wood that can be bought in Sweden is birch, in the form of planks cut from the trunk. Curly-grained birch grows sparsely here but in recent years it is being planted and grown for commercial purposes.

It is important that you decide how you would like the pattern of the grain to appear on the knife handle before sawing your curly-grained root.

4 – Sawn at a right angle to the outer shape of the root.

5 – Sawn horizontally.

If you would like the pattern to appear as dots and rings, the piece should be sawn at right angles to the trunk (photo 4). If you prefer a winding, light and dark pattern, the wood for your knife handle should be cut in the same vertical plane as the trunk (photo 5).

There is also stabilized (i.e., infused with epoxy in a vacuum) curly-grained wood available which you can purchase online, otherwise you can send off your own block of wood for stabilizing to a specialized company.

The Leather

Leather for the Sheath

The top section of the Sami-style knife sheath is made of leather and the bottom section is made of antler (refer to the book's cover photo). For the sheath I only use leather from a cow or moose.

The leather used for the sheath shouldn't be tanned all the way through nor should it be softened. It should be very stiff and about 1/16-inch to 5/64-inch (1.5 to 2-mm) thick. The characteristics of home tanned leather can be quite different from leather produced in a tannery.

Cow

Cow hide is firm and durable. The leather from a 1-year-old steer is thick enough for a sheath.

Moose

Moose hide is porous and coarse-grained, but it is also durable and beautiful. Hides from a 6 to 8-month-old calf are sufficiently thick.

Reindeer

Leather from reindeer is not thick enough for a knife sheath.

Leather for the Belt Loop

The braided leather cord for the belt loop should be strong and durable. For the loop I use 1/16-inch (1.5 mm) thick softened reindeer leather. Remove the fuzz from the flesh side of the leather.

The Choice and Dressing of Hides

Sheath leather should preferably be from a young calf. This will help you avoid a lot of work making the leather thinner. The calf should not be more than 1-year-old. If you are using moose leather, it should be from a calf around the same age. For the Sami-style twisted belt loop (page 63), it is best to use reindeer leather or a similarly thin leather.

The Parts of a Hide

Hide is composed of hair, epidermis, cutis, connective tissue, and fatty tissue. When the hide is tanned the cutis is called "grain."

Preservation

If you can't start working on the hide within a few hours after the time of skinning, the hide will have to be preserved. The two best options are salting or drying. The best type of salt is plain, non-iodized salt, available in bulk. Do not use rock salt as it can cause "burn" spots on the hide.

If you have done a thorough skinning job and removed the meat and sinews from the hide, it can be preserved immediately, without additional work, and the other procedures including dehairing, scraping, tanning, etc., can be done at a later date.

Salting a Hide

Salting should be done at least twice if the hide is going to be stored for a long period. The salt must be applied exclusively to the flesh side of the hide.

Keep the first application of salt on the hide for only one day, then brush off all the salt, dispose of the used salt, and leave the hide for 24 hours before treating it the second time. The amount of salt that will cover the hide in the first application should correspond to about 10% of the weight of the hide. For the second treatment, about 3 to 4 times more salt should be used.

The next step is to fold the salted hide the correct way for storage; flesh side to flesh side, hair side to hair side. Begin by spreading the hide out completely with the flesh side up (i.e., hair side to the ground). Take the left side of the hide and fold it over to the middle of the hide. Now do the same with the right side so the two sides meet in the middle.

Next take the small neck section and fold it over in the direction of the belly. Do not fold the whole top section of the hide over, just the neck section. Now do the same with the small rump section of the hide. Fold it over in the direction of the belly. In the next step we fold the hide completely in half from neck to rump. After this you can continue folding the hide as you please.

It should now be stored in a paper sack or similar porous material. A salted hide can be stored for up to one year.

Drying a Hide

The hide should be stretched and nailed on a well ventilated, shady wall with the flesh side facing out. The hide will shrink a great deal during drying, especially across the back, so it shouldn't be too tightly stretched when nailed for drying. When the hide has dried it can be stored indoors. Beware of birds, mice, rats, cats and other creatures as they can damage the hide when it is drying.

Note: The procedures below are the same for either a fresh hide or a preserved hide.

Dehairing

I will describe three methods. All are based on getting the process of decomposition started in order to loosen the hair. All the methods result in a bad smell, so rubber gloves are recommended, especially if you have cuts or scratches, or if you are sensitive to the smell on your hands.

1. In Water (a simple method)

Outdoors in open water, the sea or a river or stream. Put the hide with the hair facing up and tie it so it won't float away. The hide can also be weighted down with stones at the bottom. However, this pre-supposes that the bottom is fairly clean and free from mud. This method takes from one week to a month depending on the temperature of the water. A deerskin in 62° F (17° C) water takes about two weeks and a moose skin longer.

2. In Snow

Bury the hide under the snow with at least 12 inches (30 cm) of snow both over and under it. The hair side should be facing down. Keep it covered with snow as long as possible (i.e. the entire winter). If the hair doesn't loosen when the snow has melted away the process has to be immediately continued in water.

3. Using Soap

Apply a thin coating of soft soap on the flesh-side of the hide. Fold the hide in the same way as for salting. Put it in a covered container. For the first 2-3 days, the hide should be removed daily and unfolded to expose it to air, and then put away again, thereby keeping the decomposition process running. Moisten it with soft soap and water if the hide feels dry.

Check every day to determine how firmly the hair is attached. The hair should loosen easily when you try to pull away a wisp. Normally this will take 5-10 days depending on the temperature of the storage container. If the hair only becomes loose in limited areas when you test it, the wisp of hair should be put back and the process must be continued, otherwise blue marks will appear where the hair was removed.

The hair should be removed first and then the epidermis. The hair is best removed by hand. After that a wooden scraper should be used to remove the epidermis. If the epidermis isn't carefully removed light discolored areas will appear when tanning. The hide can be placed on a flat surface, a curved bench or a fleshing beam when the epidermis is scraped away.

Scraping the Flesh Side

Scraping is done with a blunt axe or a flesh scraper (aka a hide or pelt scraper). Scraping is easier to carry out if there is some moisture left in the hide. If the scraper slides too much the hide is too wet. Cornmeal can be spread on the hide the day before you scrape it. The meal absorbs the grease particles and excess moisture in the hide.

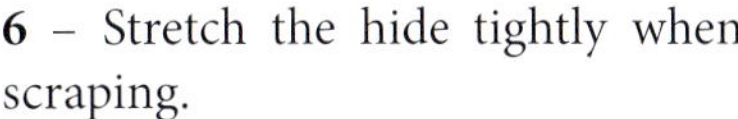

6 – Stretch the hide tightly when scraping.

The scraping process is complete when all membranes have been removed and the flesh side is even and smooth.

Scraping is tough work but it's important that it is done carefully, otherwise it will have a negative effect on the tanning process. The tanning agent will penetrate poorly where the membrane wasn't removed. Furthermore, if you scrape carefully and thoroughly there will be no "fuzz" to remove later.

Tanning

The bark to be used for tanning should be collected in the spring as its tannic acid content is highest then. First, leave the bark to dry. Then chop it into pieces of about 2-inches (5 cm) in length. Your bark decoction will be stronger if the bark is chopped. Willow is the best bark to use for leather intended for belt loops and sheath leather. Birch bark is normally used in conjunction with other kinds of bark. When birch bark is used the outer layer (the white layer) must be removed.

The Boiling Pot

The boiling pot used to make the decoction should **not** be made of iron or stainless steel. Iron absorbed by tannic acid creates black spots on the hide. The best pots for this process are made of copper. Your pot should be big enough to hold enough liquid to cover a full-size moose hide.

7 – After the first hour the hide is removed and inspected. Dehairing, epidermis removal and scraping of sinews is completed.

The Procedure

Fill the pot with the chopped bark. Add about a cup (7-8 ounces/200 ml) of coarse salt and fill the pot up with water almost to the brim. The water you use must not be chlorinated or ferrous. Boil the bark for 1 hour then let the temperature of your brew decrease to 85°F (30° C).

If the hide is very thick like the hide from an adult moose, the bark can be kept in your brew otherwise it can be removed from the decoction using a strainer.

A hide that has been dried must first be soaked before you begin tanning. The salt must be cleaned off a salted hide. Excellent results are obtained when an old bark decoction is used for the first hour and a new stronger decoction is used afterwards.

For the bath you can either use your boiling pot if it's big enough, or a separate container (e.g., a plastic barrel). Put the hide in the brew and keep stirring it around for the first hour. If you don't stir it the hide may become unevenly colored and hard to tan because the pores will get clogged with the larger particles in your tanning brew.

If there are some uncolored spots on the hide it's an indication that the epidermis wasn't fully removed before the tanning started. Correct this immediately and then put the hide back into the decoction again. Stir the hide each half hour during the first four hours. Take it out and examine it once more. Then put the hide in a new decoction bath. Use the same procedure as above when boiling a new batch of tanning solution, with the difference that this time the old decoction can be used as a base when boiling a new batch.

The total tanning time is determined by cutting a piece of the hide and examining the cut. Leather that is to be used for the sheath (i.e., hard or stiff leather) should have a thin untanned white band in the middle where the solution has not yet penetrated.

Leather to be used for other purposes, where softer leather is needed, should be tanned all the way through. A thick hide can take up to a month to tan. A reindeer hide can take 1-2 weeks.

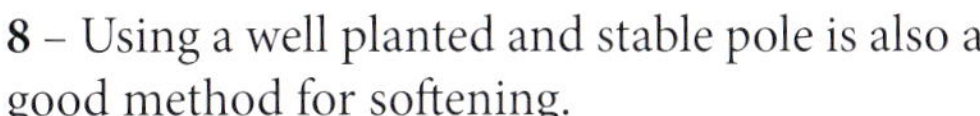

8 – Using a well planted and stable pole is also a good method for softening.

Softening

NOTE: Softening is not done on leather intended for the sheath (which needs to be stiff).

Softening is the next step after the hide is removed from the tanning decoction and has been drying for some time. Softening is done at regular intervals until the hide is dry and soft. The hide should be worked on with the flesh side facing out. The key to the softening process is to stretch the hide taut in all directions, from top to bottom and from left to right. Softening can be done on a tightly strung rope or on a rack. You can also wrap the hide around a wooden pole (or a clean saw-horse), pull it taut, and then repeat this on another section of the hide until you are done.

Dyeing

Your leather will have a light brown color from the tanning solution. It can now be dyed in different shades of reddish-brown using alder bark. Note that the pigment is in the alder's inner bark. The leather shouldn't be completely dry but should have a uniform amount of moisture when the dyeing is done.

The strongest pigments are in the alder's root, especially during the spring. Let the bark dry, sand away the gray part of the bark and then grind the remaining bark in a nut grinder. Mix the powder with hot water and you will end up with a porridge-like substance. When the bark porridge has cooled off rub it into the leather until the desired shade is obtained. It takes approximately 7 ounces (200 ml) to dye a reindeer skin.

The Blade

The Sami-style knife has a hidden tapering tang. Forging a knife blade is a science in itself. Because so many excellent books are available on this subject, I do not cover blade forging or grinding in this book. However, I would like to offer some general advice regarding the choice of a blade if you are not making your own.

The steel should not be too hard for this work knife, or it will chip or break when it hits bone or hard wood. On the other hand, it shouldn't be too soft, as it would dull too quickly (but would be easy to sharpen).

Stainless steel blades are difficult to sharpen if you use a standard grindstone. But if you are persistent it will get as sharp as a carbon steel blade. A type of blade that is a little more expensive but is very durable and maintains its edge is made from powdered stainless steel.

Through the years I've usually used hand wrought blades made by nearby blacksmiths. Knife blades are commonly produced locally in the north of Sweden where I live. Where there is no local blacksmith they can easily be ordered on the internet from retailers.

In this book I refer to the part of the handle facing the same side as the cutting edge of the blade as the handle's belly and the opposite side, the spine.

If you order a blade blank the tang should at least be 4-1/2-inches (115 mm) long. We will use the end of the tang, which must not be less than 1/8-inch (3 mm) wide at the end, to make a rivet in the handle's end cap. The tang's thickness should be as uniform as possible. It can become slightly narrower as it extends from the blade, but it must never be thicker than the blade. If that were the case it would need to be filed or ground down to the same thickness as the rest of the tang.

In addition, you should not be able to see any gap or space between the blade's ricasso and the first piece of antler on the handle. This would happen if the tang's thickness was not uniform. It would be a disadvantage if the tang had the same width, belly to spine, for its entire length. The individual pieces we will use for the handle would not easily loosen when being tested on the tang while assembling the handle.

The tang should have a width, belly to spine, of at least 9/32-inch (7 mm) at the blade's ricasso which can taper down to 1/8-inch (3 mm) at the end of the tang. That's the minimum width necessary which would leave you enough material to make strong rivets and give stability to the pommel. The tang should have a uniform taper from the ricasso to the pommel end of the tang.

9 – The blade that I used for the knife described in this book was made by Pär Björkman. The length of the blade is 3-inches (75 mm). The total length of the knife is 7-1/4-inch (185 mm). The width is 3/4-inch (20 mm) at the ricasso and the thickness of the spine and the tang is 9/64-inch (3.5 mm).

Other Materials

Spacers

It is advisable to make the spacers which separate the different parts of the handle out of natural, or natural-like material. Natural material absorbs and loses moisture in almost the same way as antler or wood when it expands or shrinks. Vulcan fiber is also an excellent spacer due to its uniform thickness, and its strength. It can be found in different colors and different thicknesses. We will use Vulcan fiber for this project but I will briefly discuss other options.

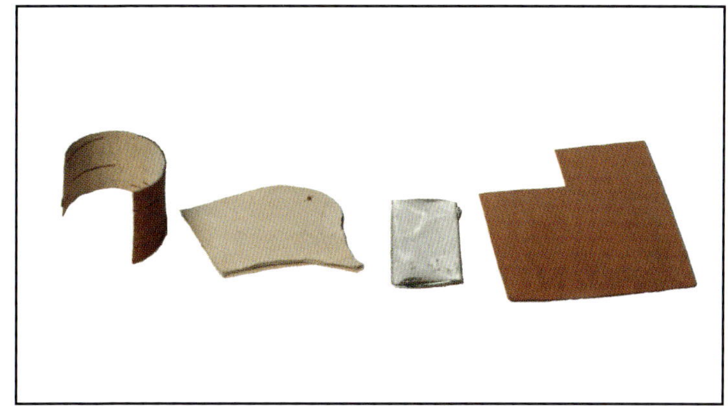

10 – From the left: birch bark, leather, tin, Vulcan fiber.

Bark/Vulcan Fiber

The purpose of using expandable spacers is to give you a good grip on the handle whether it is wet or dry. They fill out any small gaps between the different pieces of the handle. If bark is used as a spacer the light outer layer of the birch bark must be scraped away before use.

Tin

The use of tin on the handle is purely ornamental. If you want to use tin as spacer material a thickness of 3/64-inch to 5/64-inch (1-2 mm) is the most suitable. People used to think that using tin prevented witchcraft (that existed in the forest) from entering the blade.

Rivet Wire for Binding the Antler Part of the Sheath to the Leather Part

I use 5/64-inch (2 mm) brass or silver solder wire, or common rivet wire. The best is to thread a 1/16-inch (1.5 mm) hole, preparing it for a 1/16-inch or #1 (1.5 mm) silver screw. This calls for some extra tools.

A 5/64-inch or #2 (2 mm) stainless steel screw is also good to use, even if the "rivet" will be a little different in shape.

Sewing Thread

Use tarred or waxed linen cord or twine, or even thick dental floss. For very little money you can buy a sewing awl kit. These kits come with different colored thread and needles of various lengths. The needle you use should be as long as possible to avoid creating indentations on the sheath made by pressing on it with the awl.

Part II: Assembly

Preparation

I advise you to make a full-sized sketch of your design for the knife and its sheath, especially for your first attempts, in order to achieve the best, most suitable shape and proportions for you.

Generally, its shape should be gentle, with no sharp angles. Its sheath should be designed in such a way that, when hung on your belt, it will slide away from you when you sit down or when you are hiking in rough or brushy terrain.

Keep the shape of a brook trout in mind when making your knife handle. This will normally give you an esthetically pleasing and functional design.

Tools - Basic

- Hacksaw (blade with less than 18 teeth per inch).
- Rasps (coarse, flat and half-round).
- Files (flat and half-round).
- Drill (electric or hand), with bits corresponding to the thickness of the knife tang and the diameter of the rivet wire.
- Glue (two-part epoxy).
- Ball-peen hammer.
- U-shaped gouge chisel.
- Sandpaper (40, 150, 360, 600, 800,1000 grit).
- Utility knife.
- Sewing awl.
- 2 small darning needles.
- Vise.
- Screw clamps.
- File brush.

Tools - Advanced

- Band saw (14-16 teeth per inch).
- Belt Sander (Grits 40-80).
- Combined upright drill and milling machine (mill/drill press).
- Inflatable round sanders, course to extra fine, and a 5/16-inch (8 mm) file drill bit.

There is a notable difference between the hardness of curly-grained wood and antler. Because of this difference it is not recommended that you place these two materials together in the curved part of the knife handle near the pommel. If you did so, when filing the handle down, even with perfectly uniform strokes and even pressure on your file, you would not be able to avoid removing more material than intended from the softer wood material. I normally will place antler next to wood in the handle only in the section between the curve in the pommel and the blade.

NOTE: Handles made solely of antler feel cold and are unduly slippery. They will not give you a good grip.

Procedure

The handle must be completed before the sheath. It will be your guide for determining the correct size and appearance of your sheath. While the handle is best made first, the bottom part of the sheath which is made entirely of antler must be roughly planned out in advance. By doing this you will know what the best sections of antler will be to use in the handle (i.e., if you are using the same antler for both the sheath and the handle).

The Knife Handle

TIP: Never put antler directly between the jaws of a vise. This could leave marks or crack the antler. Use leather shims.

Leather is an excellent shim material to use between the jaws of the vise and the antler. It will not only prevent indentation marks, but it also provides friction for gripping the antler. There is also a rubber-faced magnetic shim that works well.

11 – This reindeer antler weighs approximately 4.4 lbs. (2 kg).

Preparation

Cut all the different pieces to be used for the handle: the sections of antler, the curly-grained wood, the spacers and the tin. For the shims I normally use 3/64-inch to 5/64-inch (1-2 mm) thick rectangular pieces of Vulcan fibre or leather. They should be larger in size than the biggest piece of antler they will protect.

The pieces of wood and antler might need to be filed or sanded where they were sawn to obtain a flat and clean 90° angle. The pieces don't have to be sanded totally smooth but any marks from sawing or rasping need to be removed.

The side of the first piece of antler which will abut the ricasso needs to be sanded perfectly smooth since it will always be visible and will not be possible to sand afterwards.

For the last piece of antler to be used—the top of the pommel—all rasp and saw marks should be filed off the surface now as well, but the antler doesn't need to be sanded at this moment.

12 – If you are a beginner it helps to make the simple tool shown here to get the pieces completely flat and uniform so that when they are placed together on the handle, they fit together snugly with no gaps. This tool is a 1/16-inch (1.5 mm) thick flat piece of iron with a hole for the antler, welded to a flat piece of iron without a hole.

The Tang

The tang on a hand-forged blade normally tapers from the blade's shoulder to the tip of the tang. If yours is not like this, your tang has to be filed down to be at least the same thickness, all the way from the shoulder, to the end of the tang.

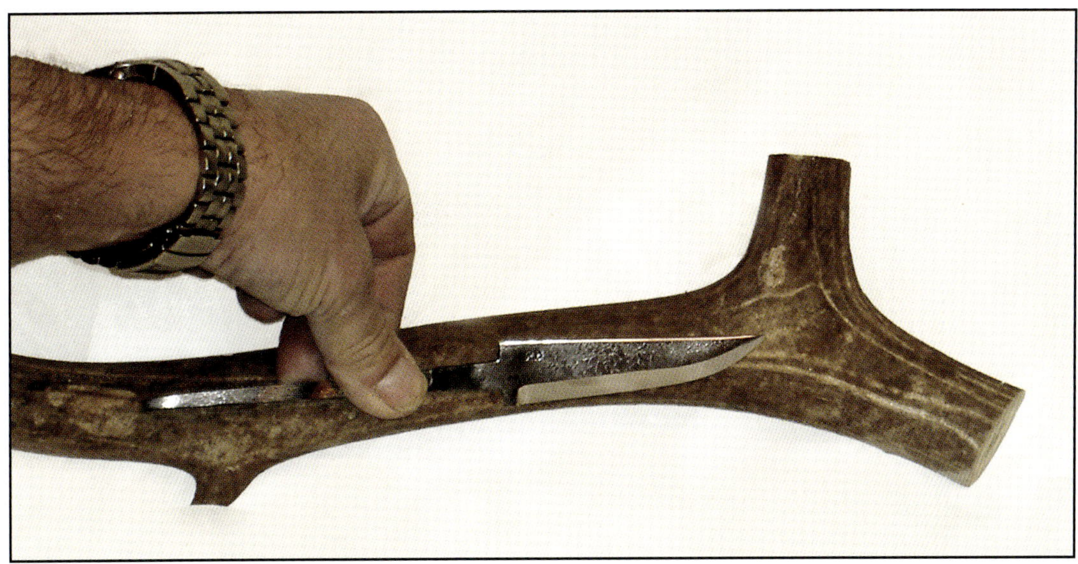

13 – With a pencil, mark off the section of antler which will be used for your sheath to determine how much of the antler will be left for the pommel.

Working on the Handle Pieces

14 – Mark the pieces you'll use for the bottom and intermediate sections.

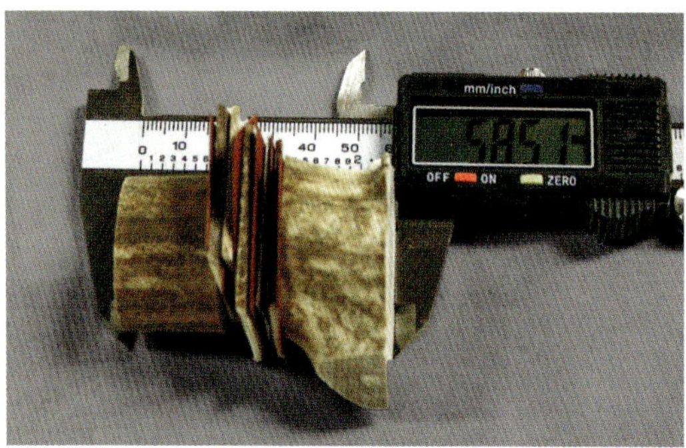

15 – Measure the total length of the combined antler pieces to determine how long the wooden section in the middle of the handle must be.

16 – The length of the curly-grained wood is adjusted to achieve a total handle length of 4-inches to 4-1/2-inches (10-11 cm). Normally this means the wood piece will be about 2-inches (5 cm) long. Put all the pieces together on top of each other, including the shims, to determine the total length of your handle.

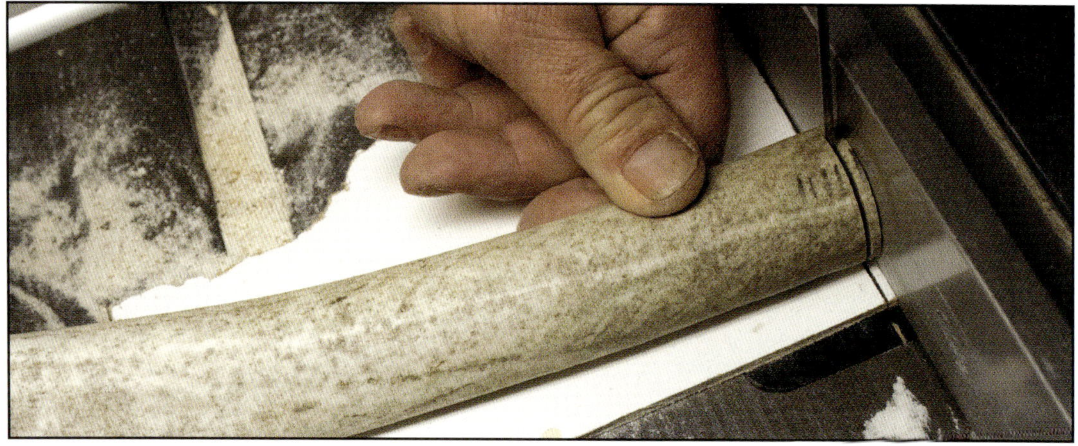

17 – If you have a band saw you'll be able to saw the pieces precisely and level enough so that sanding will not be needed afterwards. Your saw should have at least 14 teeth per inch otherwise the saw marks will be visible between the pieces.

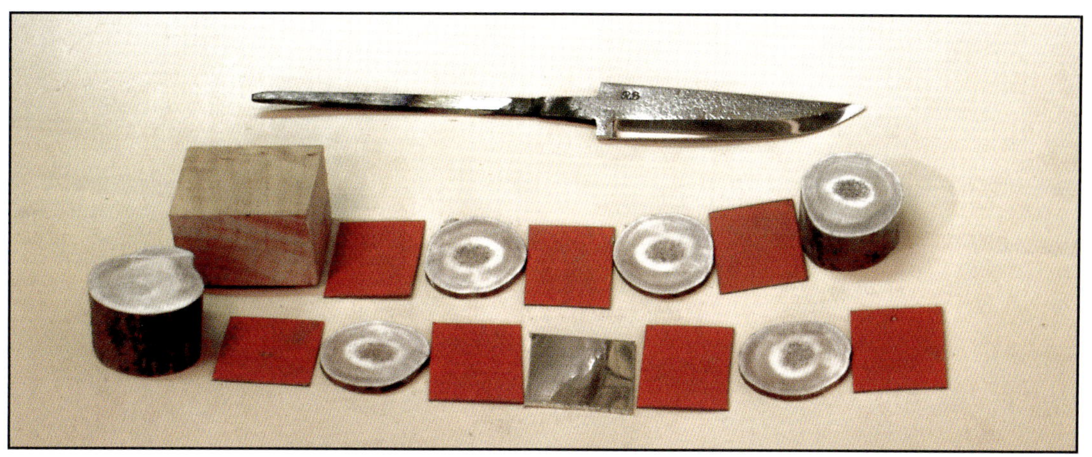

18 – All the pieces are ready for the next step.

Marking the Pieces

Every piece to be used on the handle must be marked with a pencil following a set procedure in order to have them lined up correctly and in an aesthetically pleasing way. This means that specific patterns, or differences in coloration, on a piece of antler must be lined up with the same variations on the successive piece. If the pieces are not lined up in this way, the handle will not look particularly good and its width will be different (i.e., smaller) than you had planned.

The narrowest pieces, looking from the centerline, will be the determining factor for the size.

19 – Make a pencil mark, an arrow, on the same external side of all the pieces, indicating the direction of the pommel.

Working on the Pieces

Since the tang is tapered, it is necessary to measure the thickness of the tang where each individual piece will be placed in order to choose the appropriate drill bit diameter for each piece.

When the antler marrow is dense and hard, a bit smaller in diameter than the tang thickness can be used. After drilling use a needle file to adjust the hole to the required size. When the inside of the antler is soft or porous, the diameter of the drill should be 1/64-inch (0.5 mm) less than the thickness of the tang. It is very important in the long run that your handle pieces are forced tightly onto the tang. This will increase the handle's strength which is necessary for it to hold up to the typical stress of regular use.

20 – Make a line across the center of the piece where you plan to insert the tang. This is normally the point where the marrow is widest. The orientation of the line must be the same on all remaining parts.

21 – Place the tang at a perpendicular angle to the line. Mark the width of the tang.

22 – Measure the width of the blade at its ricasso. This tang is 9/64-inch (3.47 mm).

23 – Use the drill to bore the holes for the tang to the desired width. Use needle files to make fine adjustments.

24 – Start by drilling two guide holes.

25 – Use the drill to mill material for a slot that fits the tang for both width and thickness. Use needle files to make fine adjustments.

26 – **Alternative.** You'll obtain the best results if you can use a tabletop milling machine with a coordinate table. When the milling is done (usually to half of the thickness since mills are normally too short to cover the whole depth) then drill the guide holes all the way through when the piece is still in position in the machine. Next, widen the hole from the opposite side from where you just milled.

27 – Force the piece into place by using a piece of wood with a hole in the middle.

28 – When the piece is in the correct position, make sure that there is no gap between the ricasso and the piece of antler. Make a pencil mark on the tang where the upper part of the piece ends. This will be the starting position for the next piece.

Handy Tool

To simplify forcing the pieces into place, here is a good tool to make. Cut a straight piece of birch or other hardwood, about 1-1/2-inch (40 mm) diameter and 5-inches (130 mm) long. Bore a hole through the piece which is wider than the biggest part of the tang. This tool can then be used to evenly drive the handle pieces onto the tang with a hammer.

Assembly of the Handle

TIP: Before assembling, prepare a spare shim with a large hole and a spare antler piece with the same dimensions as one of the thinner ones you're planning to use. This helps greatly if a piece is broken during assembly.

34 – Drill all pieces and test them in their "almost exact" position on the tang.

If contact adhesive is used, coat all the pieces with glue. If another type of glue is used, coat them one at a time.

I've recently started using an epoxy glue which takes 24 hours to set. This is a great advantage if something interrupts you during the assembly. Furthermore, it makes an extraordinarily strong and reliable bond.

All parts are forced into place in the proper sequence with your birch tool and a hammer. Keep an eye on the bottom (first) piece, so that it does not move out of position while forcing the others into place. When all the pieces are in position, the handle is placed in a vise with a screw clamp on the opposite side. There are different tools available on the market for this purpose.

35 – The pieces are, in this case, glued when they are pressed into position. The next piece will be a Vulcan fiber shim.

36 – After all the pieces are glued, put them into a simple clamp, that you can very easily assemble, which will keep the handle pieces tightly pressed together while the glue is drying. Make this tool with a U-shaped aluminum bar as its base, two 1/2-inch (12 mm) threaded rods attached to the base with nuts. A piece of hardwood and two nuts with washers form the top bar of the clamp. Drill a hole in the hardwood that will clear any excess tang material.

37 – After the glue dries cut the tang at a right angle approximately 1/16-inch (1.5 mm) above the top piece. File it down to 3/64-inch (1 mm).

38 – Rivet the tang flat-even with the pommel using a ball peen hammer. If it is difficult to get the rivet to expand enough, you can file it down after applying hammer blows, and then continue riveting.

Be careful when riveting! Hammer carefully. Indentation marks can damage the antler if the ball peen hammer misses when you are riveting the tang.

Shaping the Pommel

Start with a coarse file bringing the outer edge of the pommel to the desired shape. Then the rivet can be filed or ground away without damaging the outer shape of the pommel. This also gives the knife a desirable soft shape. Normally I give the top a gentle convex shape. It imparts an esthetic touch and helps, if the blade ever needs to be replaced, in removing the pieces from the handle.

39 and 40 – The curved part of the pommel ends 1/8-inch (2 mm) before reaching the butt. The edges of this last 1/8-inch should be flat around the entire circumference. This gives the pommel a more durable shape and helps in preventing it from cracking with rough usage. Use a hacksaw, coarse file or a rasp to begin shaping the wooden part of the handle.

Alternative Method

Make the pommel completely flat on top after it is riveted and its outer shape is finished. Place a 1/16-inch (1 - 1.5 mm) piece of antler, as an end cap, onto the pommel. Glue, then screw the cap onto the pommel. This will be described in more detail later.

41 – Work on the bottom part of the handle, first near the pommel, and then on the part closest to the blade, one side at a time. The handle should be the same size along the curve and at the bottom of the first piece.

I prefer to make the curved part of the pommel more acute on the cutting-edge side than on the spine side. If the curve is too pronounced on the spine side, it will be uncomfortable in some situations when using your knife. In a cross-section, the knife handle should have the form of an egg, and from the side view, it should look like a small brook trout. The long sides should taper towards the edge and be more rounded towards the back. This is a wonderfully comfortable form, as it fits the shape of the hand which holds it. It also gives you a better grip when the knife is used moving it towards yourself, for instance, when carving.

42 – Use a file or a rasp for the following. Because there is such a big difference in the hardness of the two materials it is important to file diagonally in the areas where antler and wood pieces meet. To prevent major mishaps, I prefer to hold the knife in my hand, and not in the screw vise, while filing.

The handle should be given a gentle "belly" shape in the middle. This belly needs to be 1/8-inch (2-3 mm) wider than the smallest part of the handle. The sides and handle's spine-side should also be given a belly of 1/16-inch (1-2 mm) in height. These convex surfaces are critical in order to have your knife "lock" correctly into your sheath. When you've finished shaping it, all marks from the coarse file need to be removed with a fine file.

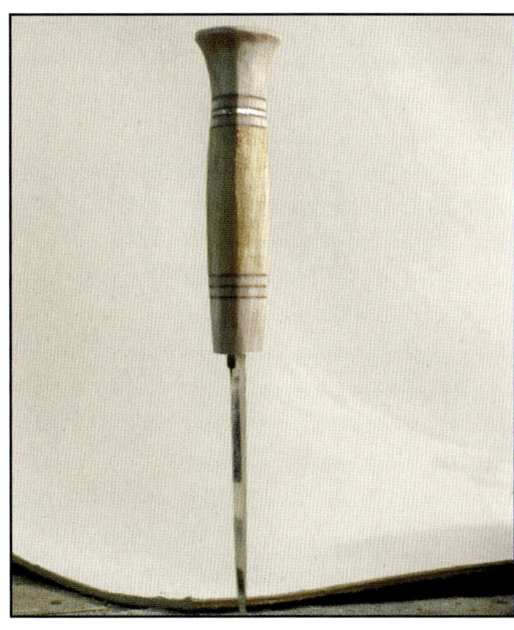

43 and **44** – The knife is now the shaped the way you want it. Sanding is now begun.

The handle should now be sanded beginning with 40 grit sandpaper working progressively up to 600 grit. Sand off all marks from the coarser sandpaper (they shouldn't be visible at all after sanding) before going to a finer grit paper. No sharp edges should be left, either on the first or the last piece.

TIP: A good progression of sandpaper grits to use for this job is 40, 120, 280, 400 and 600, but you can use what you have handy.

Sanding can be hard, time-consuming work, but what is not dealt with at this stage will be quite visible and will remain for the rest of the knife's lifetime.

TIP: Avoid sanding horizontally with the finer grits across the tin spacer. Instead, sand vertically around the circumference of the tin. This gives a better finish, and the tin particles removed while sanding will not be forced down into the wood or the antler.

When sanding is being done with 400 grit, moisten the wood with warm water. Let it dry at least one hour and then sand very gently with the next grit. This is to be continued up to the highest grit that you use. If you want to have a glossy surface you should use a buffing wheel with polishing material. If you intend to make a pattern on the antler it shouldn't be polished at this stage because your pen marks would rub off too easily from a polished surface.

45 – A tool that simplifies sanding is the inflatable flexible drum sander. The drum is pumped up as desired, and then attached to a flexible shaft. Different diameters and grits are available.

Alternative: Pommel with End Cap

It's attractive and sometimes useful to cover the top of the pommel with an end cap made from a plate of antler. Following is a way to do this and an explanation of how to shape the handle with the help of a belt sander.

TIP: To give it extra strength the piece for the end cap should come from a vertical cut of the antler and not a horizontal cut.

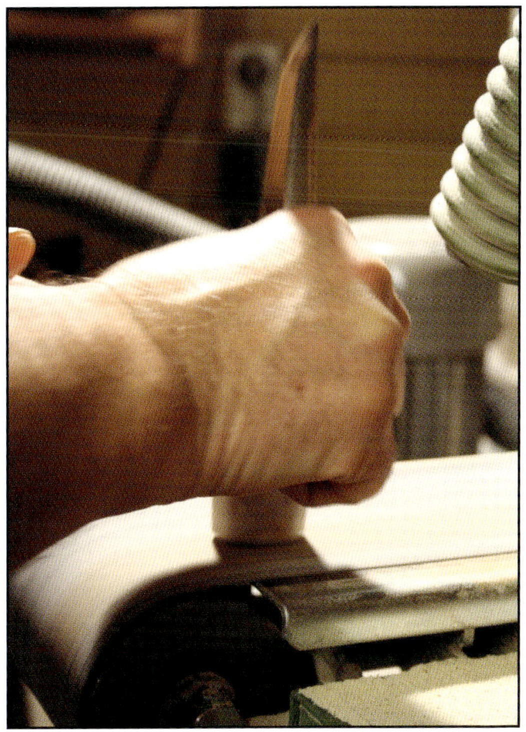

46 – Form the pommel in the shape you want it and make its butt-end completely flat. This means that the rivet also needs to be filed down flat to the same surface.

47 – As explained previously the curved part of the pommel ends 1/8-inch before reaching the butt end, and the edges of this last 1/8-inch should be flat around the entire circumference.

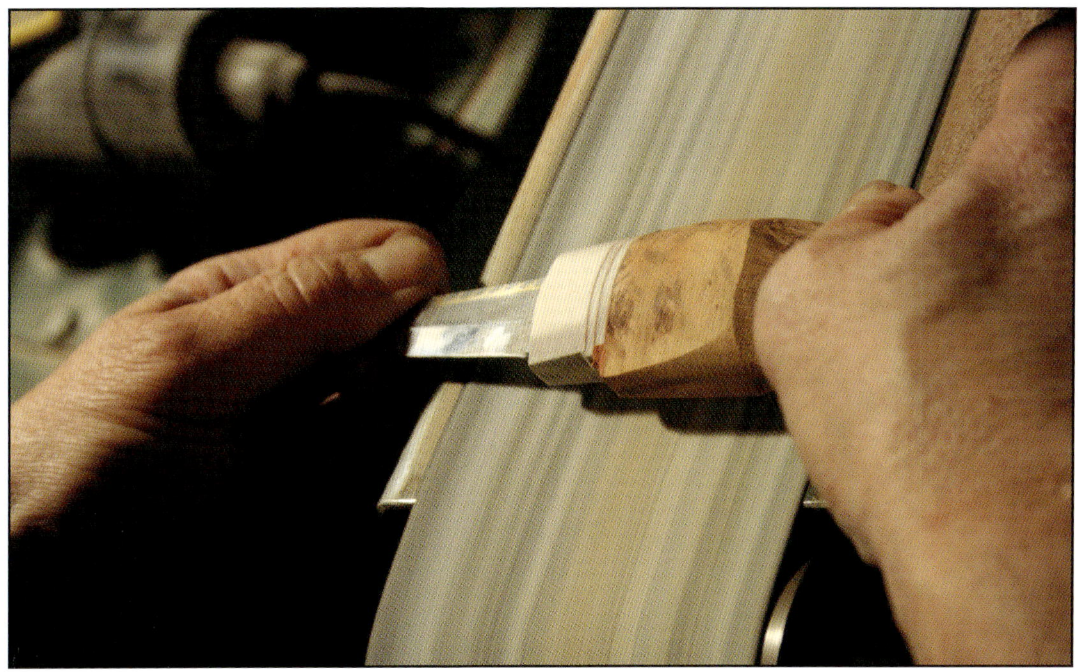

48 – The handle is made as described earlier. The only difference is that the "pommel curve" is roughly shaped the whole way around to begin with, and then the rest is shaped with a belly as previously explained.

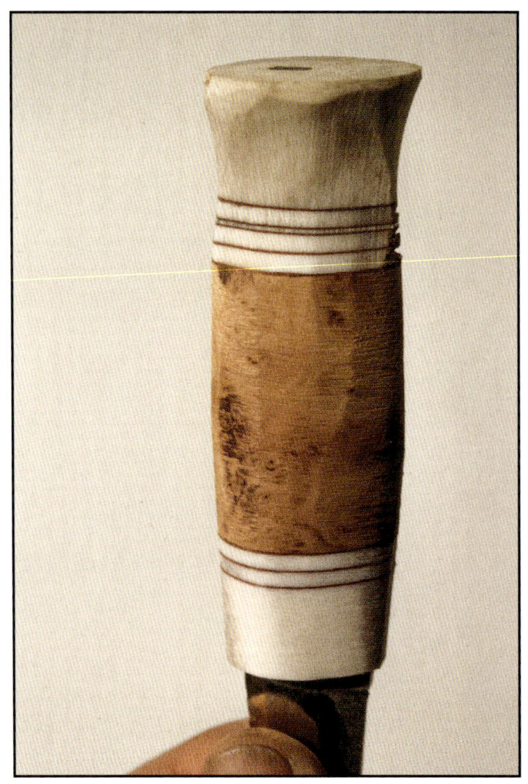

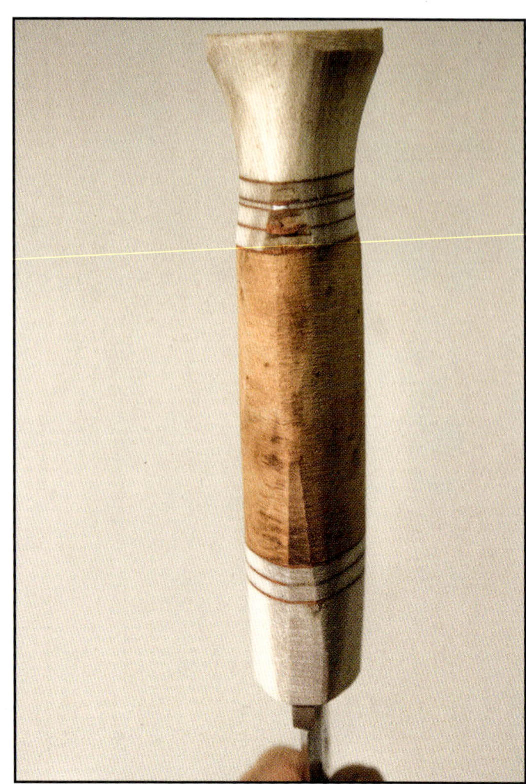

49 and **50** – Roughly shape the handle with a belt sander the same way described previously. Remember to leave a certain amount of material and to remove, **by hand**, the last portion of material using a coarse file. **Things happen very fast with a belt sander**!

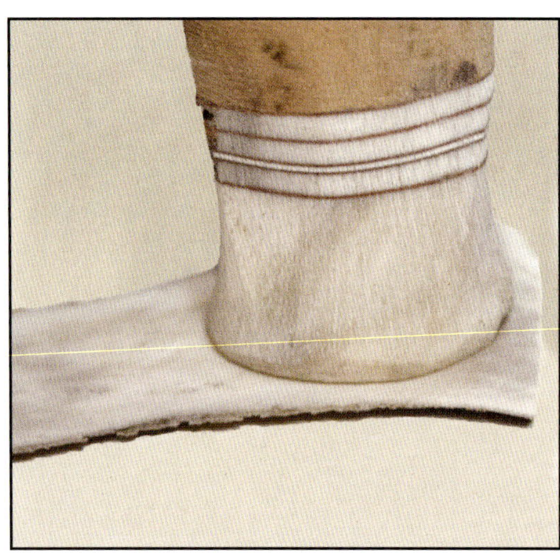

51 – The section of antler that is suitable for the cap can be taken from antler that isn't the right quality from the perspective of marrow content. The 5/64-inch (2 mm) thick plate should be slightly larger than the pommel. It must be sanded flat and smooth on the side which will be glued to the pommel.

52 – Glue the plate to the pommel. After it has hardened, screw the pommel and the plate together very gently. I use two 5/64-inch (2 mm) screws which go through the plate into the pommel. I first draw a line across the middle of the plate so the screws are correctly aligned. After this is done carefully, sand down the rim of the plate (which was slightly larger than the pommel) to the edge of the pommel.

Staining

If you're looking for more structure in the wood, and want to achieve a greater contrast, you should stain it.

I normally use oil-based leather dye for this purpose. Only use a small amount on the brush each time because this type of dye is very runny and can suddenly splash or drip on the antler and it will be hard for you to remove the splash marks. Start with yellow dye, let it dry 30 minutes, then sand softly with 600 grit. Then apply red/brown dye. Let it dry, then sand softly with 1000 grit. To finish, apply a dark brown color. When you're satisfied with the stain you've applied, dry the wood thoroughly and then sand it softly with 1200 grit.

If you think the handle became too dark or you would prefer a different contrast, you can sand off the brown stain until you get a lighter color surface and then either oil it or put yellow stain on it.

Leather dye is oil-soluble so a small amount of the color will disappear when you oil it.

The handle is now ready to be oiled.

Finishing

The wood must be finished. A time proven mixture is 50% gum spirits of turpentine and 50% boiled linseed oil. The oil will penetrate better if it's warmed up before it's applied.

TIP: Coat the threads of the linseed oil container cap with Vaseline so that the cap won't get stuck.

Raw linseed oil doesn't darken the wood as much as boiled oil. Boiled linseed oil hardens in about one week, while raw linseed oil can take up to 2 months, depending on the temperature. This method shouldn't be used on a porous antler because it will become yellow after a while if it is oiled.

The following procedure is recommended for finishing.

Apply the oil until the wood is fully saturated. Let it dry and then apply the oil again. The treatment is repeated as often as needed. There is an old bit of advice regarding the application of oil which goes:

"Apply every minute the first ten minutes, every hour the first day, and every day the first week".

After each application, all excess oil must be removed within one hour otherwise the oil will form lumps and will harden on the outside of the wood.

When the oil has dried, after about one week, it's possible to polish the surface with a sheepskin buffer. If this doesn't give you the finish you want, you can apply carnauba wax, beeswax, Danish oil, or as an alternative, gun-stock oil. Then the wood can be polished to a beautiful, glossy surface.

SAFETY WARNING: Depending on the circumstances, paper towels or rags that have been used for wiping off linseed oil—which generates heat as it dries—can spontaneously ignite. For safety reasons, put the rags in water or burn them after use.

Part III: The Sheath

The Bottom Half (Made from Antler)
Dividing the Antler in Half

NOTE: Your traditional Sami-style sheath will have two distinct parts, the bottom half which is made of antler and the top part which is made of leather.

Remember the following when choosing the section of antler for your sheath: the external side of the antler (i.e., as it was on the reindeer's head) is normally used for the external side of the sheath, and the internal side is normally used on the internal side of the sheath (i.e., the side which rubs against your pants).

The piece of antler used for the sheath must be cut down the middle. It is difficult however to determine an exact "middle" because antler is often curved both lengthwise and crosswise. This is to be expected and is not a problem.

NOTE: The antler part of your sheath will become narrower during sanding, so always start with a section of antler which is considerably wider than the blade.

Always start your cut from what will be the bottom part of your sheath, below the antler's hook, where the antler is narrowest. Because there is less antler material there to work with, this is the most delicate part of the sheath and needs the most attention. It is important that you cut directly through the middle of this part to obtain the same amount of antler on both sides of your cut in that narrow section. Your complete cut, which must always be along a straight line (but not usually perpendicular), will most probably end up to the right or to the left of the center of the top of your antler piece. This is OK and perfectly normal. In photo 56 you can see that the cut does not finish in the middle of the top part of the antler. Cuts like this work out fine because we have more antler material to work with on the wider top part. Moreover, almost an inch of the antler will be covered by the leather top-part of the sheath, so this difference will not be visible.

When you begin removing marrow and antler from the inside of the sheath halves, material will disappear from the bend where there is the least amount of antler. This means that if the cut isn't in the exact middle of the curved part, the thinner half will dictate the shape and will give you a sharper "hook".

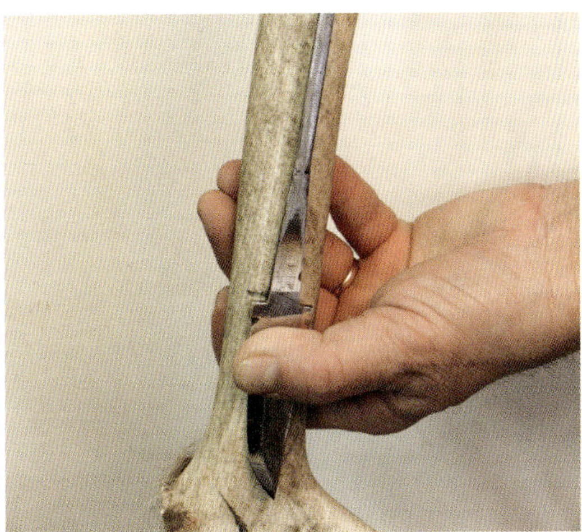

53 and **54** – Draw the line along which you will cut the antler. This will depend on which Sami style of sheath you are making. In our case it will be in the Northern Sami style, which means it will have a more pronounced hook.

Working on the Interior of the Antler Halves

55 and **56** – This piece of antler bends sideways at the front tine, as antler often does; thus the cut cannot be exactly perpendicular. The cut must be made at an angle in order to have enough antler on both sides all the way to the top. The cut must go through the center part of the antler at its narrowest part on the bottom leaving an equal amount of antler on both sides. Note that the cut will not end up going through the exact middle on the top part of the antler. As previously explained, this is perfectly normal and to be expected when you make your sheath.

When the antler sheath halves are cut, most of the marrow should be removed from the inside. This can be done first with a rasp and the rest can be sanded flat with coarse sandpaper attached to a flat piece of wood. If this isn't done, it may seem to you later that you have more hard antler material to work with than you actually do. Such a mistake can lead you to removing too much of the hard, external part of the antler and you will end up sanding right down to the marrow when you are shaping and finishing your sheath. Sanding down to the marrow will make it impossible to create a good pattern and will cause the antler to discolor with time.

57 and **58** – Draw a pencil line on the antler piece so your cut will be precise.

59 and **60** – Use a hardened fine toothed finishing saw (a high tooth count is necessary) to cut the antler in half. Use leather in the vise to protect the antler.

SAFETY WARNING: Sanding creates a lot of harmful dust so always protect yourself with a mask and use a dust collector or particle exhaust fan.

Hollowing Out the Inside

Before you make a compartment for the blade on the inside of the antler, roughly finish the outer part of the sheath. This is done now so you'll have a better grip on it when you place it in the vise when you make the compartment for the blade.

After making the compartment the play between the blade and the sheath should be such that the blade is supported along its spine but does not touch the cutting-edge curve while sliding into place. If that happened it would quickly dull the cutting edge.

61 – If this sheath half were filed any more, too much of the antler would be removed along the curve and along the entire curved side, making the shape we want impossible to obtain.

62 – The edge side of the filed sheath has a lot of antler left. The shape of the antler on this side is always rounder than on the hooked side, which is flatter.

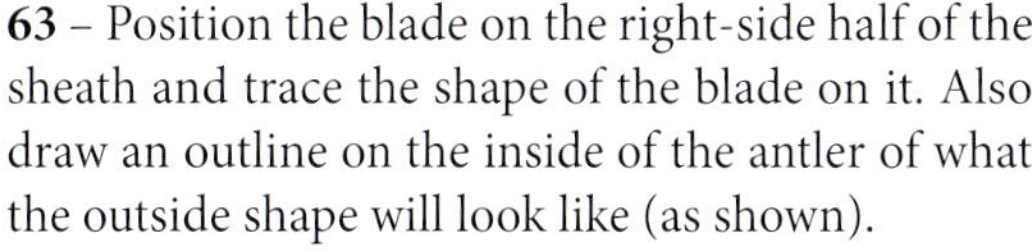

63 – Position the blade on the right-side half of the sheath and trace the shape of the blade on it. Also draw an outline on the inside of the antler of what the outside shape will look like (as shown).

64 and **65** – Draw a straight line, as illustrated, extending from the spine of the knife to the bottom of the sheath. This extension of the line will be slightly hollowed out and used for drainage.

66 – Saw a groove with a depth of half the blade's thickness plus 3/64-inch (1 mm) along the line you made.

67 – Use a U-shaped chisel to hollow out the area of the sheath inside the outline you made of the blade. Always work from top to bottom to avoid having parts of the antler breaking off at the top.

68 – Now check to see if your knife goes smoothly into the sheath. The edge should not be cutting into the antler.

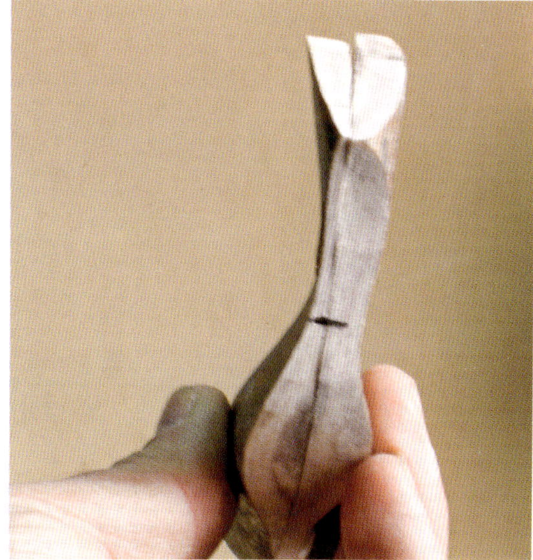

69 and **70** – Hold the two halves together and make a pencil mark from the groove on the top part of the antler across to the same exact spot on the other half of the sheath, then do the same thing on the bottom part of the antler.

71 – Now draw a straight line between the marks you just made on the top and the bottom of the second sheath half.

72 – Finish the compartment for the blade so that it is hollowed out at the blade point and has a smooth inclination over to the groove, which will be used for drainage.

An Alternative Method Using Power Tools

73 and **74** – Use a band saw with a 12 or 14 teeth-per-inch blade. For the work you see in these photos I used a band saw that is a bit too narrow. Normally I use a blade that is at least 1/2-inch (12 mm) wide which helps me to saw straight when needed.

75 – Use a belt sander with a 40-80 grit belt. Be aware of the fact that the belt "eats" the material extremely quickly. Moreover, as the belt gets duller it can "burn" the antler. This means that the heat generated by an over-worn belt will harden the surface of the antler so that it becomes difficult to draw patterns on it.

76 – Place the knife in position and trace the outline of the blade.

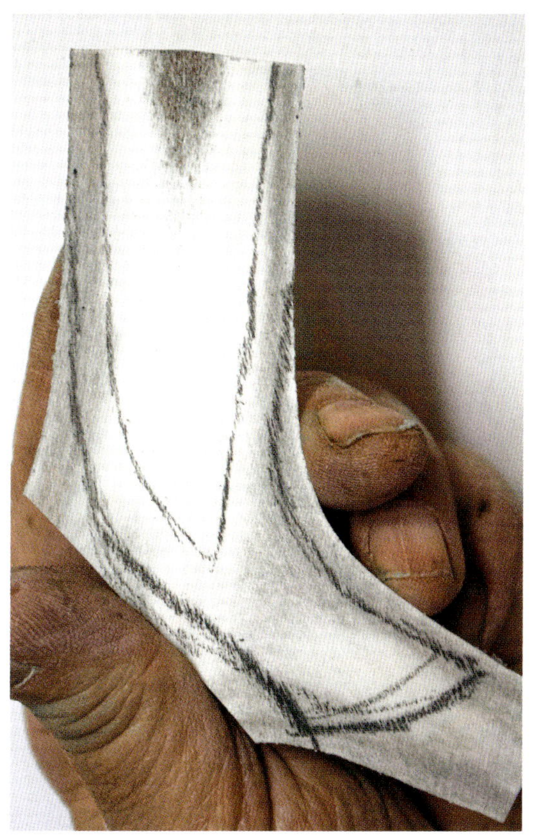

77 and **78** – Draw the outline of the definitive shape of your sheath.

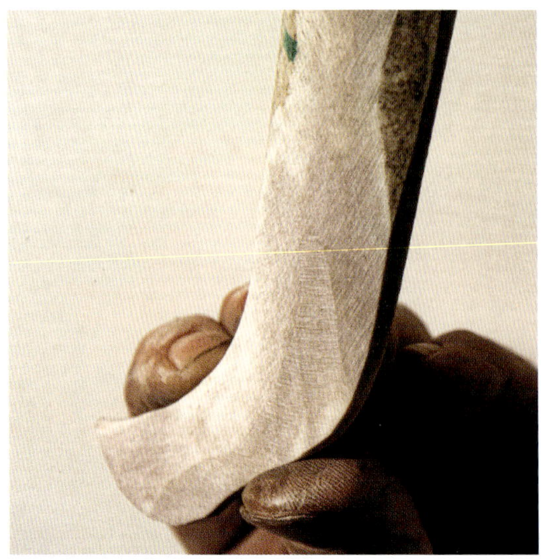

79 and **80** – Roughly shape with a saw, rasp, or both the external part of one of the sheath halves. Next, trace the outline of that shape on the other sheath half and roughly finish the exterior part of that side as well.

81 – Draw the form of the knife blade and the drainage groove. There should be a smooth transition from the knife compartment to the drainage furrow.

82 and **83** – Use a grinding bit with a cylindrical shape. Use the shaft of the bit to guide you on how deep to mill on the spine side. Don't hollow it out that deeply on the cutting edge side. When making the transition to the drainage hole use a bit with rounded tip.

84 and **85** – Hold the sheath halves together. Make pencil marks on the right-hand half of the sheath indicating the points where the hollowed-out section begins and ends on the corresponding left-hand half of the sheath. Do this both on the top and the bottom (the drainage hole) of the halves as the photos illustrate. This blade has a rectangular shoulder, which is why the hole is made rectangular as well.

86 – Hold the halves together and put the knife into the sheath. Sketch the circumference of the knife making your outline 5/64-inch (2 mm) wider. The purpose of this is illustrated in photos 93 and 94.

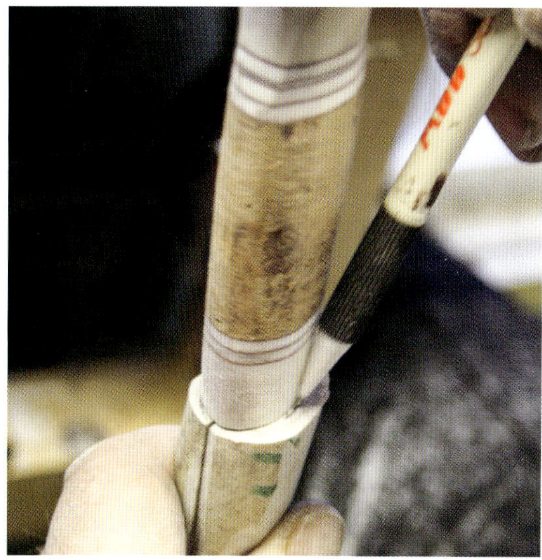

87 and **88** – On the external half of the sheath (i.e. the right-hand side) mark the points in pencil where you will drill holes for the screw rivets, then drill them with a #53, 0.0595-inch (1.5 mm) bit.

89 – Clamp the two halves together and drill only one hole on the other sheath half as shown.

90 – Put glue on the two halves. Insert a 1/16-inch (1.5 mm) pin to guide the two halves together into the correct position while the glue dries.

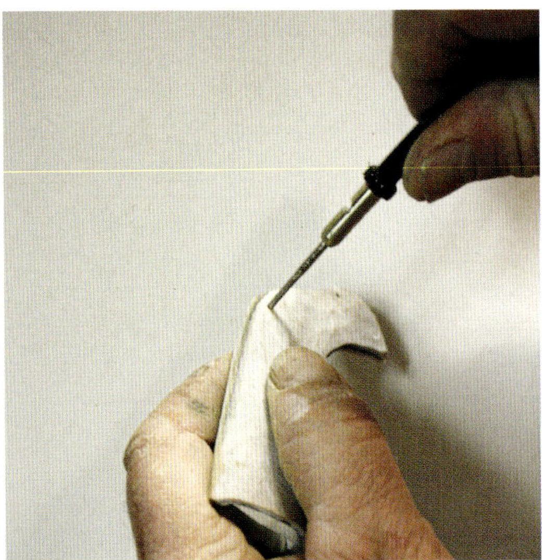

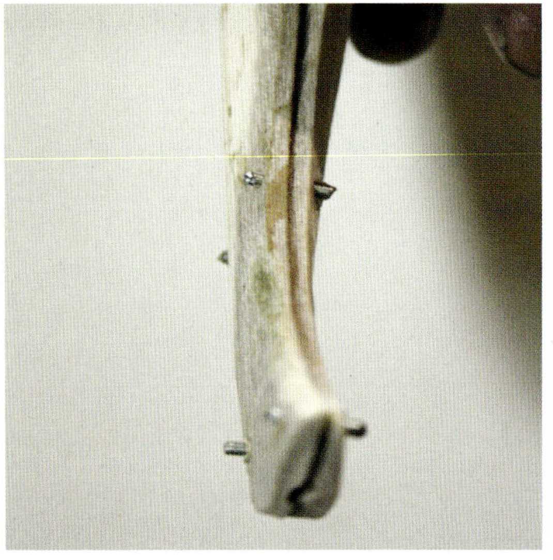

91 and **92** – After the glue has completely dried, drill all the holes and thread them for 5/64-inch (2 mm) screws. Put some instant glue into each hole before putting the screws in. Then trim the screws as closely as possible to the sheath.

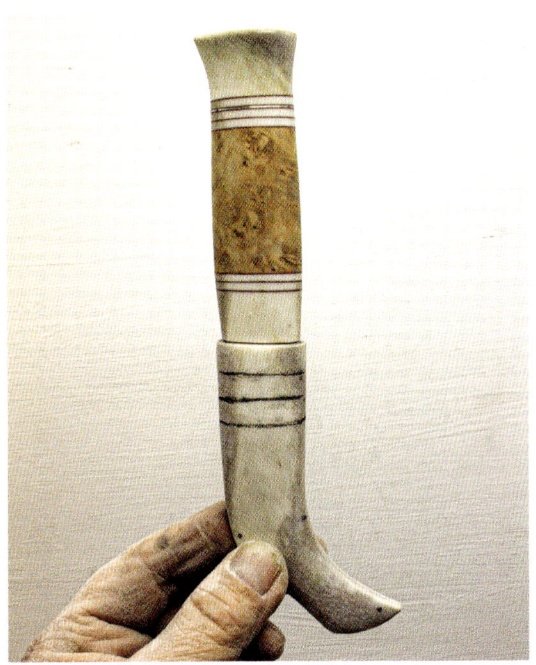

93 and **94** – Put the two halves together so they match as much as possible the outline you made on the sheath (5/64-inch (2 mm), from the knife's blade). Draw marks where the rivets will be inserted and use a grinding bit on your Dremel (i.e. rotary tool) to make these as described in the following pages as the 'standard' way. An alternative way will also be explained.

Shaping the Outside of the Sheath

Put the knife in the sheath. The knife needs to be square with the top of the two sheath halves, otherwise the typical "click" sound will not be that distinct when the knife is put into the sheath.

Finish shaping the rest of the sheath half. The only fixed measurement is the form of the knife, which you outlined on the sheath.

95 – When the halves are hollowed out the opening for the knife should be beveled. This is done to prevent your blade point from sticking into a flat antler surface when it's put into the sheath. With a beveled opening the blade will be guided smoothly down into the sheath.

96 – Hold the two halves together carefully. Place the butt of the handle on the antler and trace a line around the bottom of the knife on the top of the sheath. The line should be approximately 5/64-inch (2 mm) wider than the exact circumference of the handle's butt.

97 – Draw a line along the inside of the "outer half" of the sheath. This is to provide fixed points for when you shape the outside of your sheath.

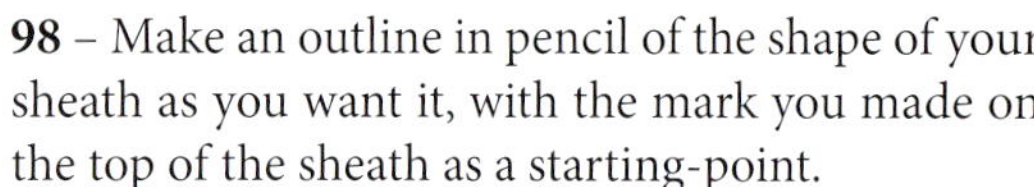

98 – Make an outline in pencil of the shape of your sheath as you want it, with the mark you made on the top of the sheath as a starting-point.

99 – Shape (with a file, rasp or belt grinder) the sides using the lines you drew as guides. As you can see the sheath is a little bit bigger than the blade. When you make the fitting for attaching the top leather part of the sheath, 3/64-inch (1 mm) of this material will be removed.

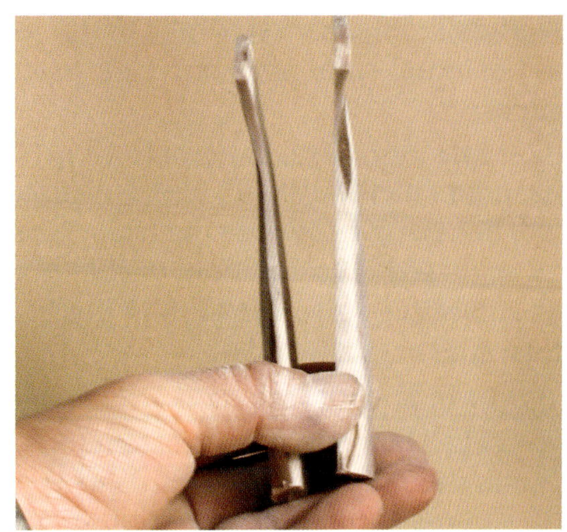

100 – Make the halves as narrow as you like in the lower part but not up to the point where you risk sanding them right down to the marrow. On the left is the half from the cutting edge side and to the right the spine side.

If you feel confident about shaping the other sheath half to match the first, then simply proceed the same way as with the first half.

If you don't do this then it is best only to work on the other half where the rivets will be placed. It should be brought to its final width. The thickness should be the same for the two halves. Now it is possible to rivet the halves together and complete the rest of the sheath without damaging or destroying the rivets.

Standard Assembly of the Sheath

Mark the spots where the rivet(s) will go on the inside of the first sheath half you made. The upper rivet(s) should be placed crosswise and should be the same distance from where the edge of the sheath will be. Place one or two rivets, depending on the length of the sheath's hook, in the middle of the hook.

On one sheath half drill all the holes with the same diameter as the rivet. Now place the halves together. The saw grooves on each half should align with each other.

101 – If the section of the sheath after the hook is long, I recommend using two rivets to keep the halves from warping over time.

110 and **111** – The ridges are 3/64 to 5/64-inch (1-2 mm).

The purpose of the ridges is to keep the leather securely attached to the antler part of the sheath. The leather will be stitched tightly around the antler section and thus, it won't wear out through abrasion.

The sheath is sanded the same way you did with the handle.

The Top Half (Made from Leather)

Measuring the Leather

The leather will shrink as your hide dries after tanning. Different parts of the hide will shrink more than other parts. For example, the skin on the belly shrinks more than the skin on the back. There is less shrinkage along the length of the hide than across it.

It's hard to determine what part of the hide your piece of leather came from if you haven't tanned it yourself. You won't know exactly how much it will shrink once it is attached to the antler section of your sheath. Leather will expand when wet and shrink as it dries therefore it is useful to soak the leather, measure it in both directions, let it dry, then measure it again.

Doing this you will get a better feeling for the correct size for the rectangular piece of leather to cut out for your sheath and also how to take into account and compensate for shrinking when you sew it. Leather which you purchase will normally shrink approximately 1/8-inch (3 mm) lengthwise from damp to dry.

The piece of leather should be attached to the sheath oriented so that it will shrink less in a vertical direction down the knife handle than across and around the handle. Remember that there is less shrinkage along the length of the hide than across it. When dry, the leather part of your sheath should be approximately 1-3/16-inch (2 cm) above the belly of the knife.

Cutting the Leather

Cut out a rectangular piece of leather. Make sure the long sides are parallel to each other.

The length of the leather part of the sheath should extend from 1-inch to 1-3/16-inches beyond the belly of the knife handle. You should add 3/8-inch to 5/8-inch (1 - 1.5 cm) extra to the length of the leather if you intend to fold over and tuck in (to the inside of the sheath) the top part of the leather achieving a "rounded" opening for the knife (explained later on).

The width of the leather should be the circumference of your handle's belly plus about 2-3/8-inches (6 cm).

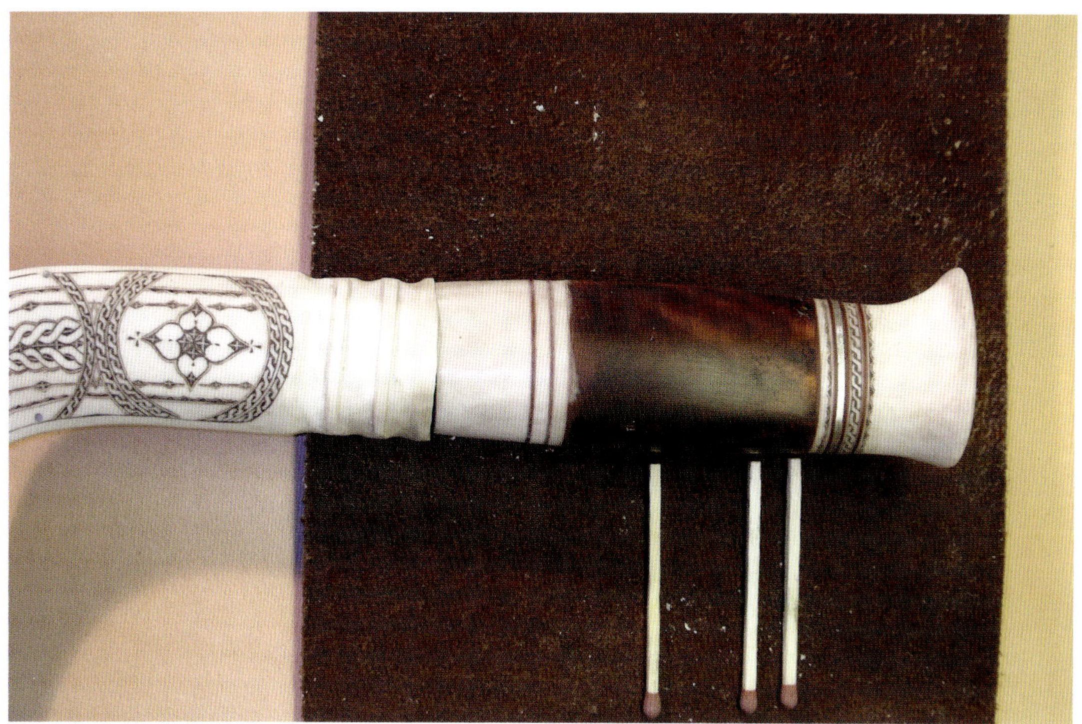

112 – Put your knife inside the antler part of the sheath and place it on the rectangular piece of leather with the butt of the handle at the edge of the leather. Draw three marks (represented here with matches). The top mark is where you will cut the leather if you want to fold the top over. The next mark indicates the height after the top of the leather is folded over and sewn, after the leather has dried. This mark also indicates where to cut it if you don't intend to fold it. This position will change depending on how much the leather shrinks. It is better to make it too far up than too far down. The mark at the bottom indicates where the middle of the belly is on the knife handle.

Soaking

Before you start sewing, the leather needs to be soaked, otherwise it would be impossible to sew. Soaking should not be done longer than necessary. When the leather starts to soften and can easily be bent, it is time to stop soaking it. How long this takes depends on how the leather was tanned. If the leather is about 5/64-inch (2 mm) thick and comes from a tannery, the time might be 10-30 minutes. Hand-tanned leather can take several hours. Keep the leather in a plastic bag for 1 hour to get it soaked all the way through, then let the leather dry in the open air for 30 minutes before sewing.

TIP: Don't use warm water!! The water you use can't be warmer than 98.6° F (37° C), otherwise your leather will be ruined.

Thickness

The top and bottom parts of the leather should be thinned down (see the piece of leather under the knife in the photo below) to about 5/64-inch (2 mm). For the top part, which will be folded over, start the thinning about 3/4-inch (2 cm) from the top. Do this with a very sharp knife. If you have a belt sander it's very simple to use when the leather is dry. Make sure you do this not only on the top part but also the bottom where the leather will be attached to the antler. Make the bottom part progressively thinner to obtain a gradual transition to the antler part.

Alternative Procedure

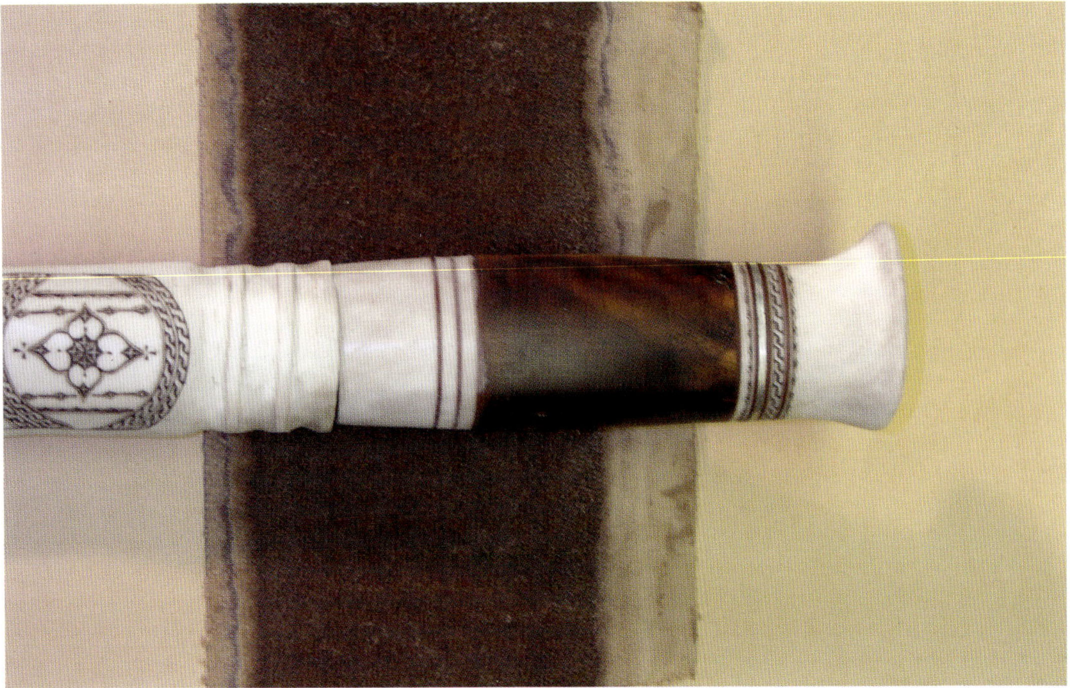

113 – This piece of leather under the knife is prepared so it will have a folded top. The light parts have been thinned.

If you choose to have a rounded top on the leather, you should proceed as follows: the height of your piece of leather should be about 3/8-inch (1 cm) higher than in the previous method. The leather will need to be thinned starting about 3/4-inch (2 cm) from the top. It should be about 3/64-inch (1 mm) thick and the last few fractions of an inch should be reduced almost to nothing. Fold over to the inside 3/4-inch (2 cm) of the leather.

You can also glue the folded part, while it is still damp, with an instant glue. Folding makes the opening of the sheath more attractive and makes it stronger for attaching a twisted leather loop which we'll make shortly.

114 – Make the first stitch with your awl approximately 5/32-inch (4 mm) from the bottom if the leather is very thin in the lowest part. The higher up the first stitch is made the more the leather will shrink to a V-shape on the back side. Make stiches on each side. Since the leather has been thinned and will be sewn tight, it will be stretched a great deal as it dries.

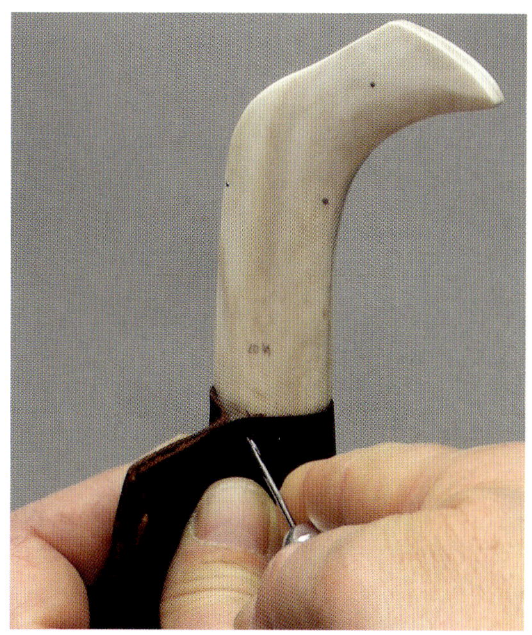

115 and **116** – As you are sewing it stretch out the lower part of the leather which is in contact with the antler. Don't stretch the leather which extends above the antler. It should be easy to hold the leather in place with your fingertips while doing this. See Figure 1, page 61, for further instructions.

117 – From the belly of the knife handle the seam should be sewn straight up to the top. Continue with the seam over the top as shown.

118 – Continue making stitches along the original seam or make a seam around the hole for the belt loop (see next section). Don't use a cutting-needle at this stage. Finish with a flat knot.

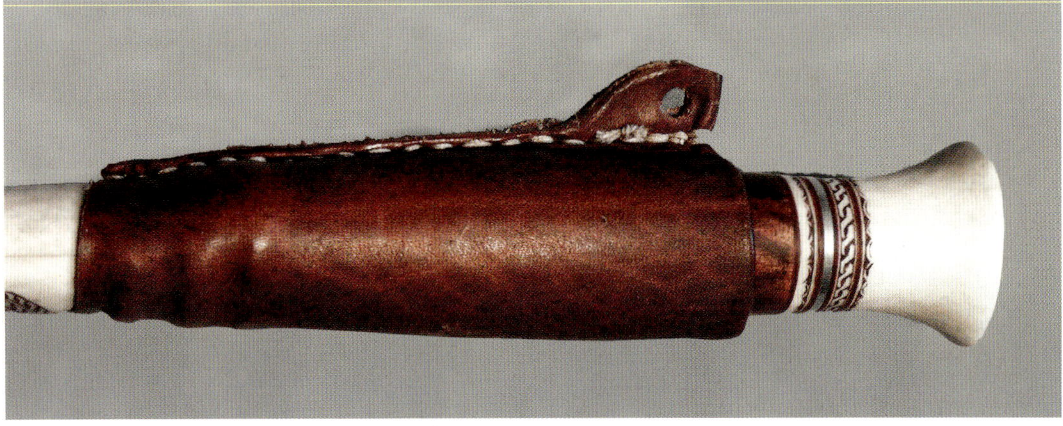

119 – Cut away approximately 3/64-inch (1 mm) of the excess leather above outside the seam but leave some extra leather around the hole for the belt loop as illustrated.

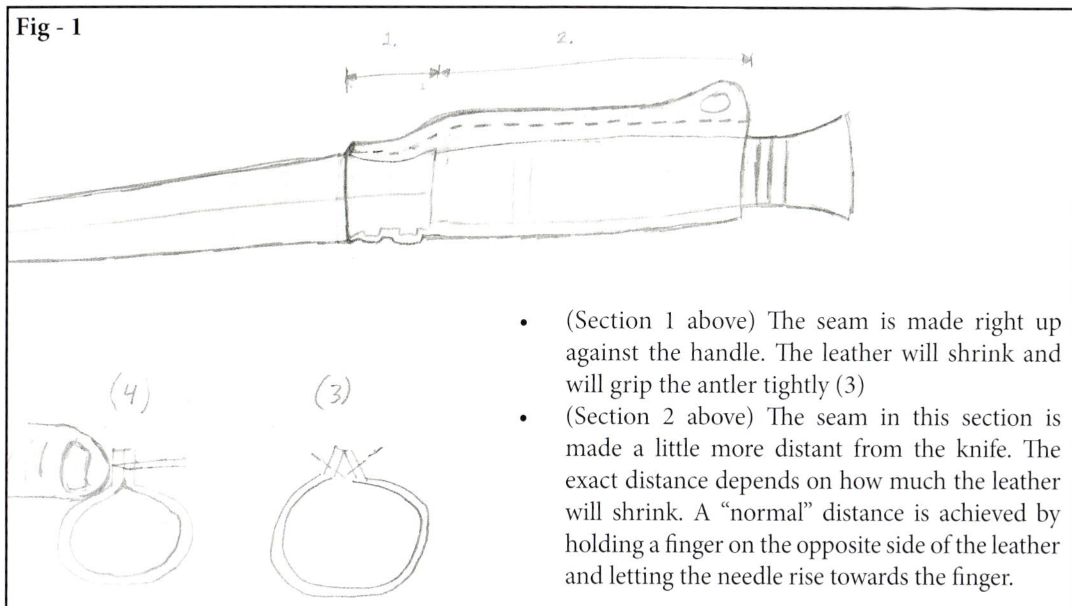

120 – To soften and smooth out the seam rub it back and forth with a piece of antler fashioned as follows. A 5/32-inch (4 mm) hole is drilled horizontally through a piece of antler, then the piece is cut into half horizontally through the middle of the hole thus making a channel (see drawing below). The leather must be moist when doing this! See photo to the right.

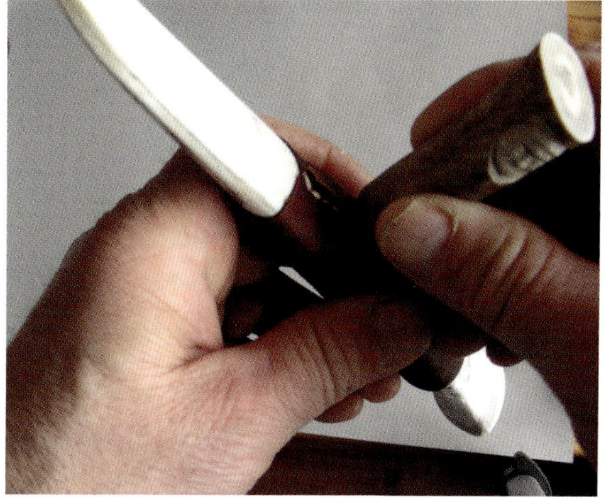

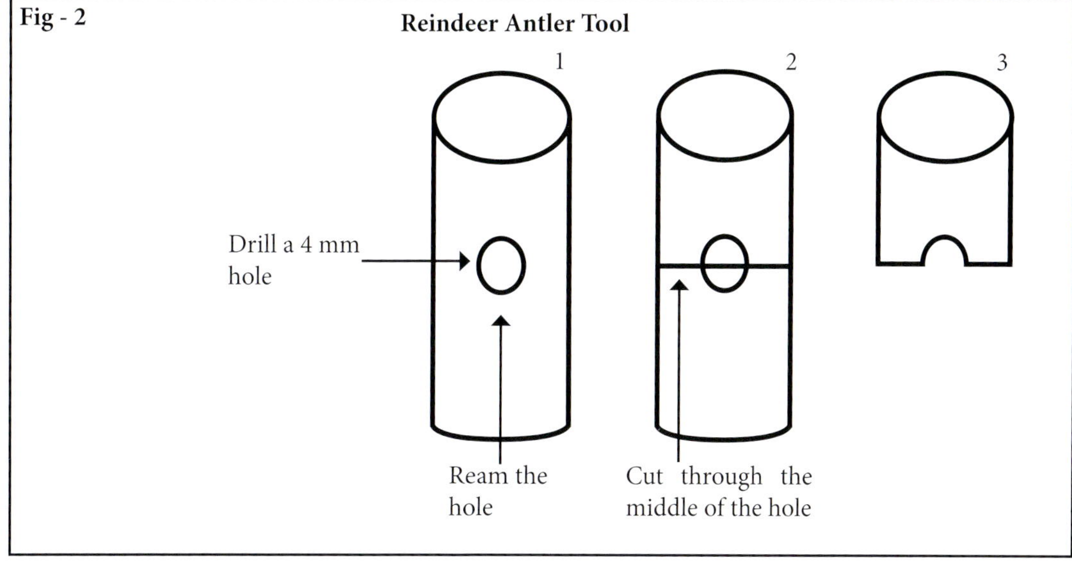

The Seam

Make a shoemaker's seam with waxed or tarred linen thread. Use a cutting-needle on one end of the thread, and a thin darning-needle on the other.

You can also use thin darning-needles on both ends of the thread. You can block the thread by sticking the needle through it. An alternative to using two needles is for you to use a hand sewing awl.

Fold the leather around the knife to make sure the seam runs down the exact middle on the internal side (i.e. legside) and also make sure the bottom part of the leather is parallel to the top part of the leather. If you are a novice and don't know how to keep an equal distance between stitches, it's a good idea to mark where each stitch will go beforehand.

Normally an awl is used to make the holes on both sides of the leather. Make the holes for one stitch at a time, in order to maintain the same distance between stitches and maintain the same (straight) direction.

In case a cutting-needle is used, this should be run through the leather first to avoid cutting the thread. Seams tend to twist away from the side where the first awl stitch is made so it's good to switch from the side where you made the first one. Cut or punch a hole (photo 119) for the twisted leather loop (photos 121–124).

It's good to put edge wax on the edge of the leather after it has been rubbed. Mold and shape the leather around the external side of the sheath using a modeling tool without sharp edges. You can emboss the leather with a pattern while it's still wet.

This type of leather ("Sami" leather) can't be shaped, as, for example, leather that's used for ordinary leather knife sheaths. The leather can be colored with leather dye regardless of whether it is dry or still wet.

Alternative

Using a sewing awl will simplify your sewing. Thread can be bought in different colors.

Drying the Leather

When the leather has dried for about 24 hours at room temperature, it's time to pull the knife out of the sheath. If it's stuck, the leather will have to be soaked again to draw the knife out.

The best thing to do at this point would be to use a new piece of sheath leather. The second best is to completely soak the leather and wrap a plastic bag twice round the knife handle, put it back in the sheath, and let it dry for at least two days. The disadvantage with this procedure is that in the future, when the knife is exposed to rain and then dries, without using a plastic bag it might be hard to remove the knife from your sheath.

Finishing the Leather Surface

When the leather has dried, it can be coated with regular wax.

The Belt Loop

Cut a strip from a thin piece of soft leather. The width of the strip you make will depend on the thickness of the leather you have. Normally you would cut a strip about 5/8-inch (15 mm) wide if the leather has a maximum thickness of 1/16-inch (1.5 mm). It should be about 16-inches (40 cm) long.

Cut the piece into 3 strips, joined at the end (i.e., don't cut them all the way to the end). Stop cutting the three strips approximately 3/8-inch (10 mm) from the end (photo 121).

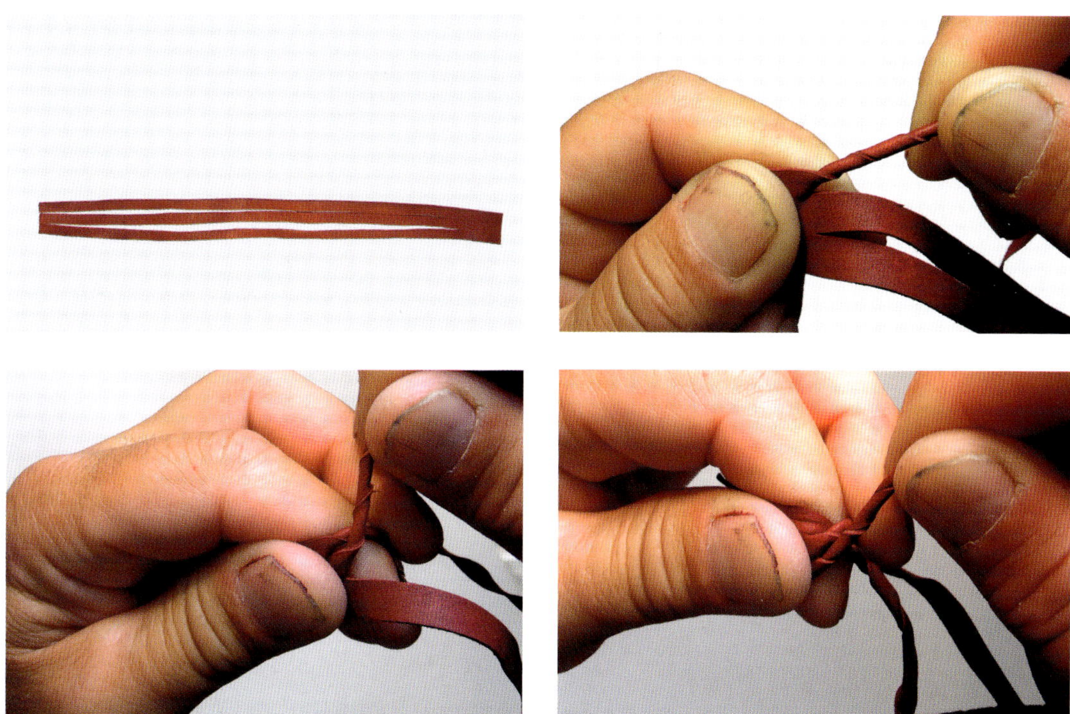

121–122–123–124 – Hold the un-cut end in your left-hand between your thumb and forefinger and let the leather strips point to the right, side by side. Fold one leather strip in the form of a U with the top surface outwards (always).
Twist the strip most distant from you counter-clockwise with your right thumb and right forefinger. Stretch it out and hold it with your left middle finger.
Twist the next strip counterclockwise, stretch it and put it over the first, clockwise. Hold this one now, instead of the first one, with your left middle finger.
Twist the third strip in the same way and put it over the first two. Start with the first one again and continue until you have the whole piece twisted. After that, soak the ends and press them together.

Fig - 3

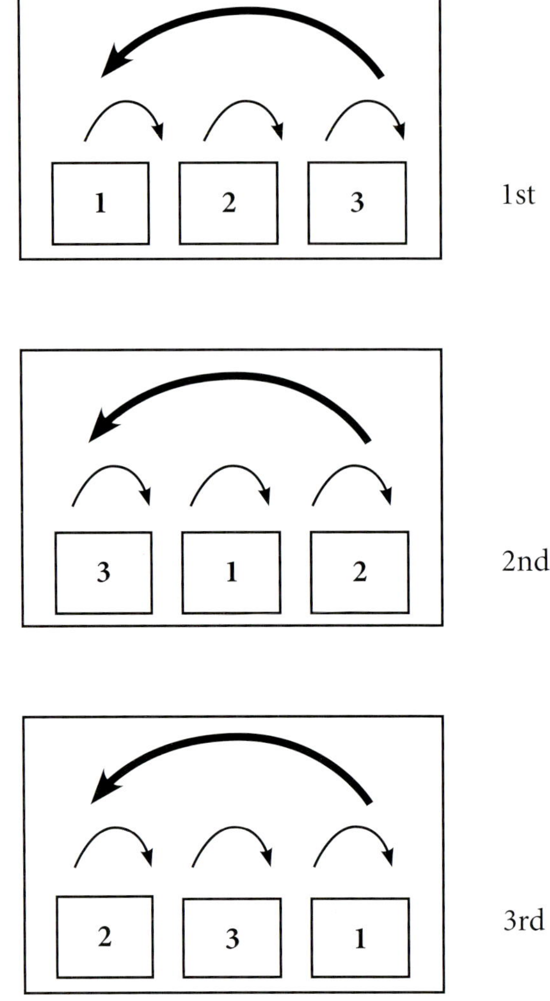

The three steps illustrated. After step 3 start from step 1 again and so on.

Patterning

The last step in our Sami-style knife sheath project is to carve a pattern on the external side of the antler and then to dye it. Carving a design in antler or bone is also referred to as scrimshawing. This is the most time-consuming part of our entire project. Many excellent books and videos are available which teach patterning and scrimshawing. I recommend that you refer to one of them to supplement the basic information given in this section. This is a complex art and takes time and practice to learn, but it will add a new and rewarding dimension to your knifemaking skills. A few simple procedures will now be explained. Several traditional Sami-style patterns are also provided which will give you a very handsome sheath.

TIP: Practice your patterns and carving and coloring techniques first on spare or scrap pieces of antler before you attempt to do this for the first time on your sheath or knife handle.

It is much easier to make a pattern in reindeer antler than in wood because there are no fibers "steering" your scrimshawing knife in the antler.
The following will be necessary for you to obtain the best possible results:

- A very sharp scrimshawing knife (not a wood carving knife).
- An exact sketch of the pattern on graph paper.
- Moisture in the surface of the antler.
- Good lighting conditions.
- A "gentle hand" (i.e. never cut deeply!).
- Enough time and lots of patience.

Patterning will normally take 75% of your total project time, and that is with just a normal amount of patterning on the sheath and the handle. Patterning on the curved handle is very time consuming and is more difficult than doing it on a flat surface.

If the antler is too dry when you begin, you will need to wrap a damp paper towel around the antler 30 minutes in advance.

If the antler is too smooth take 600 grit sandpaper to the antler and roughen it up slightly.

TIP: A common mistake among beginners is to cut the pattern too deep into the antler. Keep your cuts shallow! Curved surfaces, like the handle, are difficult to pattern since it is hard to keep the knife at the correct angle all the time. The knife tends to slip. Pay attention. Go slowly.

125 – A basic technique with scrimshawing is to always force the knife away from yourself and use your thumb as a lever.

Tools

126 – A bright, portable halogen or led lamp; a pivoting vise to use when you are unable to hold the knife or sheath in your hand while patterning; a leather cushion on which to position your knife while patterning.

127 – Patterning/scrimshawing knives of various widths and angles.

Your patterning knives should be made of hard steel. Make sure they are knives made for scrimshawing. Woodcarving knives are not hard enough. Lately I have started to use powder steel knives like ATS 34 (US equivalent, 154-CM) or RWL 34. Knives can also be made from "tool steel" or from an old threading tap. It is essential that your knives are very sharp before you begin using them. Reasonably good sharpness is not sufficient. Have some 1200 grit sandpaper at hand to maintain blade edge sharpness while patterning.

If your pattern has many curved lines, it is best to use a knife with an angle of about 35°. To simplify "edge stitching" and to keep your patterning knife sharp it is a good idea to make a separate knife for this job which looks like a flat 5/64-inch (2 mm) screwdriver.

Check your knife's sharpness now and then by lightly stroking the knife's edge on your fingernail. If it's still sharp enough, the knife should stick to your nail.

Sketching

Use a 1/8-inch (3 mm) H lead pencil. In case the antler's surface is polished you will have to dull it a bit, otherwise it will be too difficult to draw on it. Use a small plastic transparent ruler; the flexible kind, and which has fractions of an inch (or mm) clearly indicated to mark out your pattern.
If the lines in your pattern are very close to each other or are very small, it is a good idea to sketch the pattern as a "negative". This means marking out what's going to be left, instead of marking out what is going to be cut away.

In a zigzag pattern, this will mean that the black zigzag sketch is left untouched and only the uncolored part will be cut away.

128 – I start by making a sketch showing how I intend to arrange the patterns

A Basket Weave Pattern

The basket weave pattern isn't difficult to sketch or cut when the system for the design is understood.

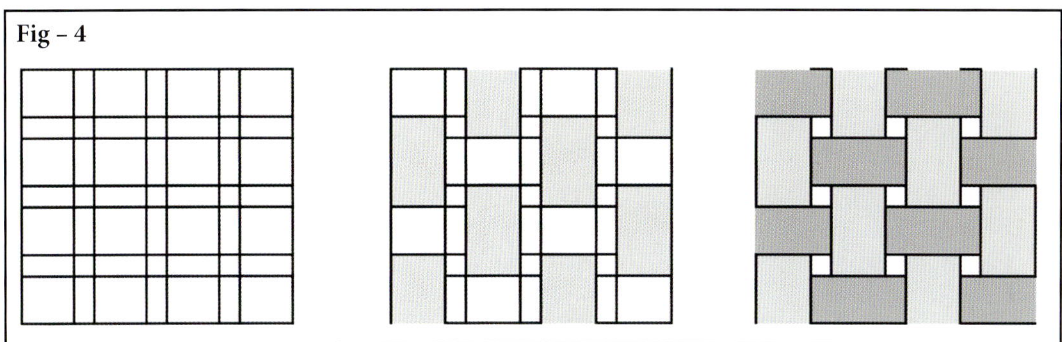

1) Start drawing the lines using a 3 to 1 ratio both vertically and horizontally. You can scale it up or down with the same approximate relationship (4.5 to 1.5 is a good start). **2)** Use an angled rubber eraser to remove the lines underneath the light gray colored parts (in this sketch). **3)** In the same way erase the lines underneath the dark gray colored parts.

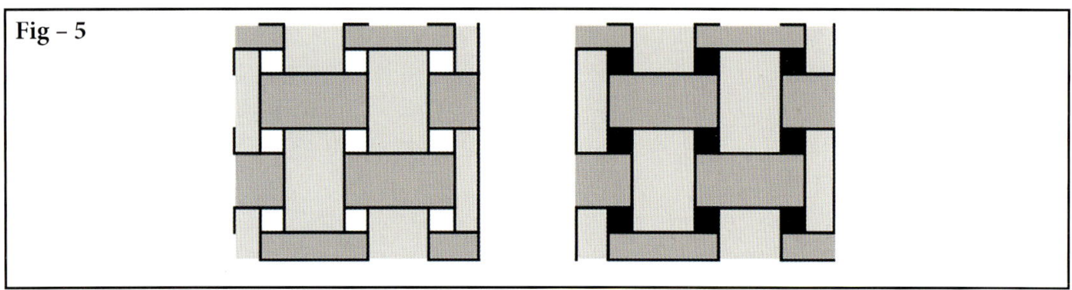

Fig – 5

I prefer to start and finish the pattern with a half-sized basket band as shown in the sketch. Doing this you avoid having a black "empty" space on the border of your pattern. You can simplify your sketching and cutting jobs if you blacken the "empty" spaces between the bands.

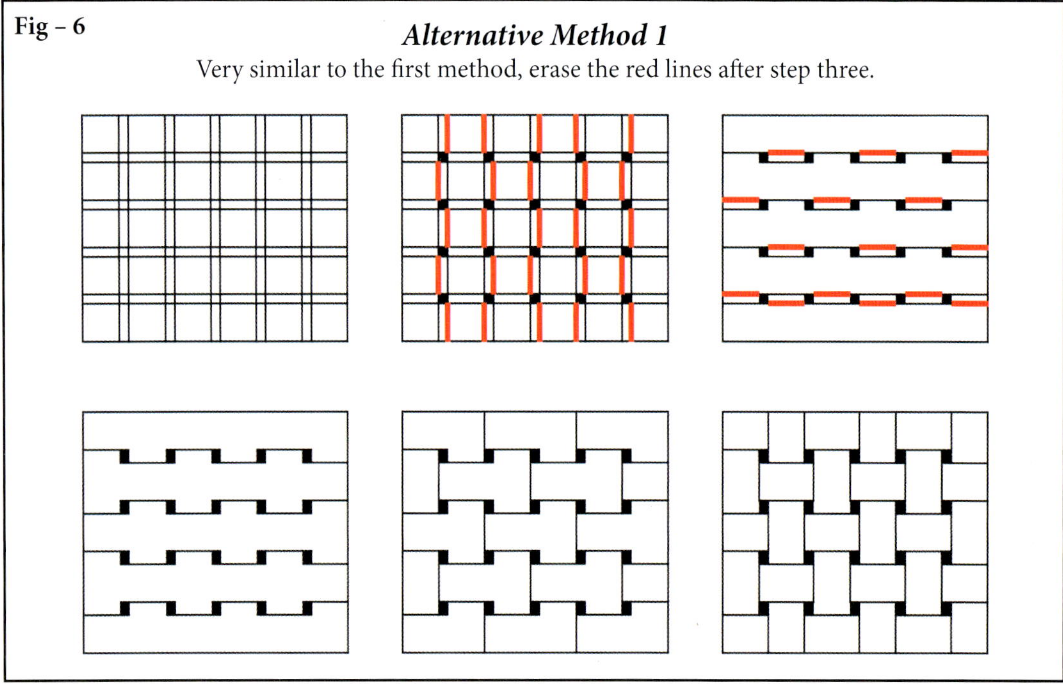

Fig – 6

Alternative Method 1

Very similar to the first method, erase the red lines after step three.

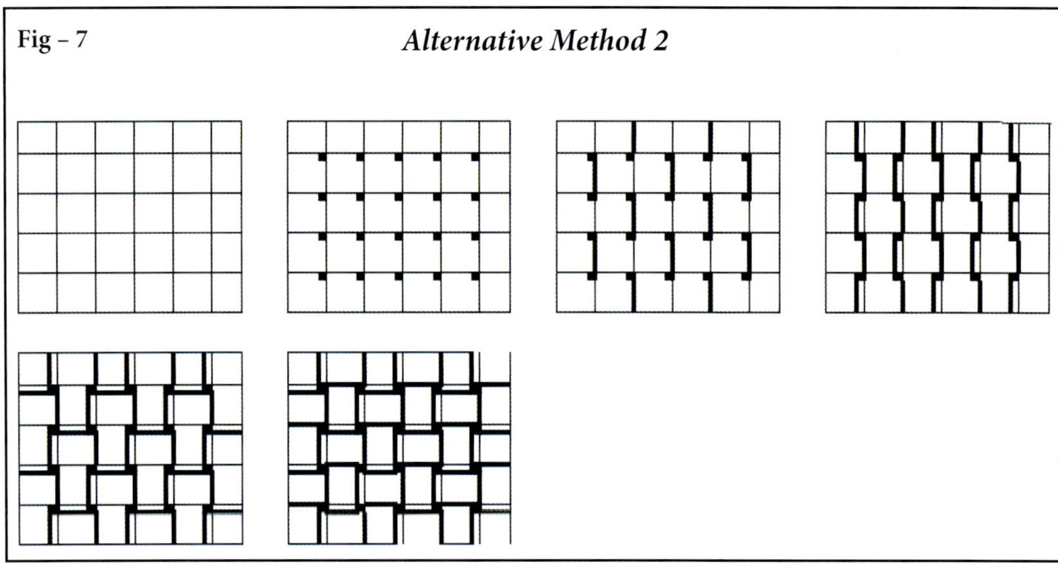

Fig – 7

Alternative Method 2

Procedures

All lines, straight or curved, should be cut twice from two angles, to achieve a V-cut.

Never cut deep! If you do, this will adversely affect the result. Practice your cutting by applying only very light pressure on your knife. This is difficult to do, especially after a while when we automatically—but mistakenly—start putting more pressure on the knife.

If you want to make a line more dominant, make the V wider and a **tiny** bit deeper as well, but I'm speaking about a **very** small difference in depth.

You should begin the second cut which will form the V by starting it from the bottom of the first cut and moving your knife forward very carefully. If you do this correctly a small antler shaving should loosen when forcing the knife forward.

If you are making a complicated pattern it may be hard to know which lines to cut from which side (i.e. from the "outside" or "inside"). Because of this problem I try to be methodical and so I cut all lines from the "outside" of the pattern first. When patterning a ring it is easy to understand what the outside lines are, but when cutting other patterns this has to be "translated" to that specific pattern.

As a beginner it is important to make your cuts straight. When patterning a curved line this entails moving or turning the antler instead of your patterning knife. Carving will be easier if the antler is not clamped into a vise while patterning.

TIP: Cut your straight lines with a knife which has a long straight cutting edge. The longer edge will help to keep the lines straight.

Use a good light which shines from behind you on your left side if you are right-handed.

Sometimes it can be useful to change the direction of the light to highlight the shadow from the first cut.

When your scrimshawing knife is pushed down in the opposite side of the V you should feel a definite "snap".

I use different patterning procedures depending on the proportions of the pattern, but I always make an estimate of the dimensions of each separate pattern to be sure there will be enough space to complete each one and that its proportions will be attractive.

131 – Note how the braid rises from below the squares and ends "underneath" the successive braid.

132 – The braid design is completed and the border between the patterns is cut.

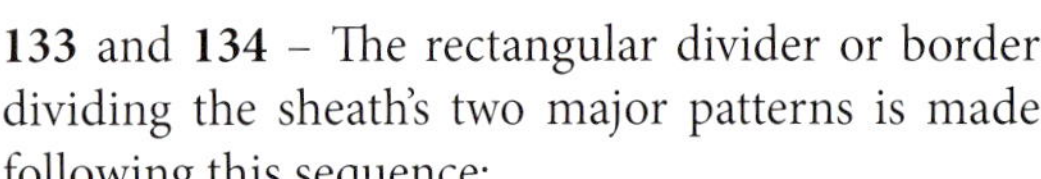

133 and **134** – The rectangular divider or border dividing the sheath's two major patterns is made following this sequence:

1) Divide the space into squares.

2) Draw a center line.

3) Sketch the braid from the centerline both upwards and downwards

4) Sketch the black background and the S-shaped designs within the border lines

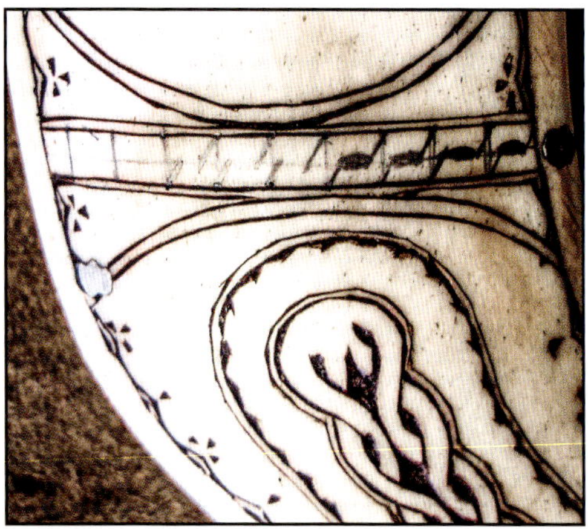

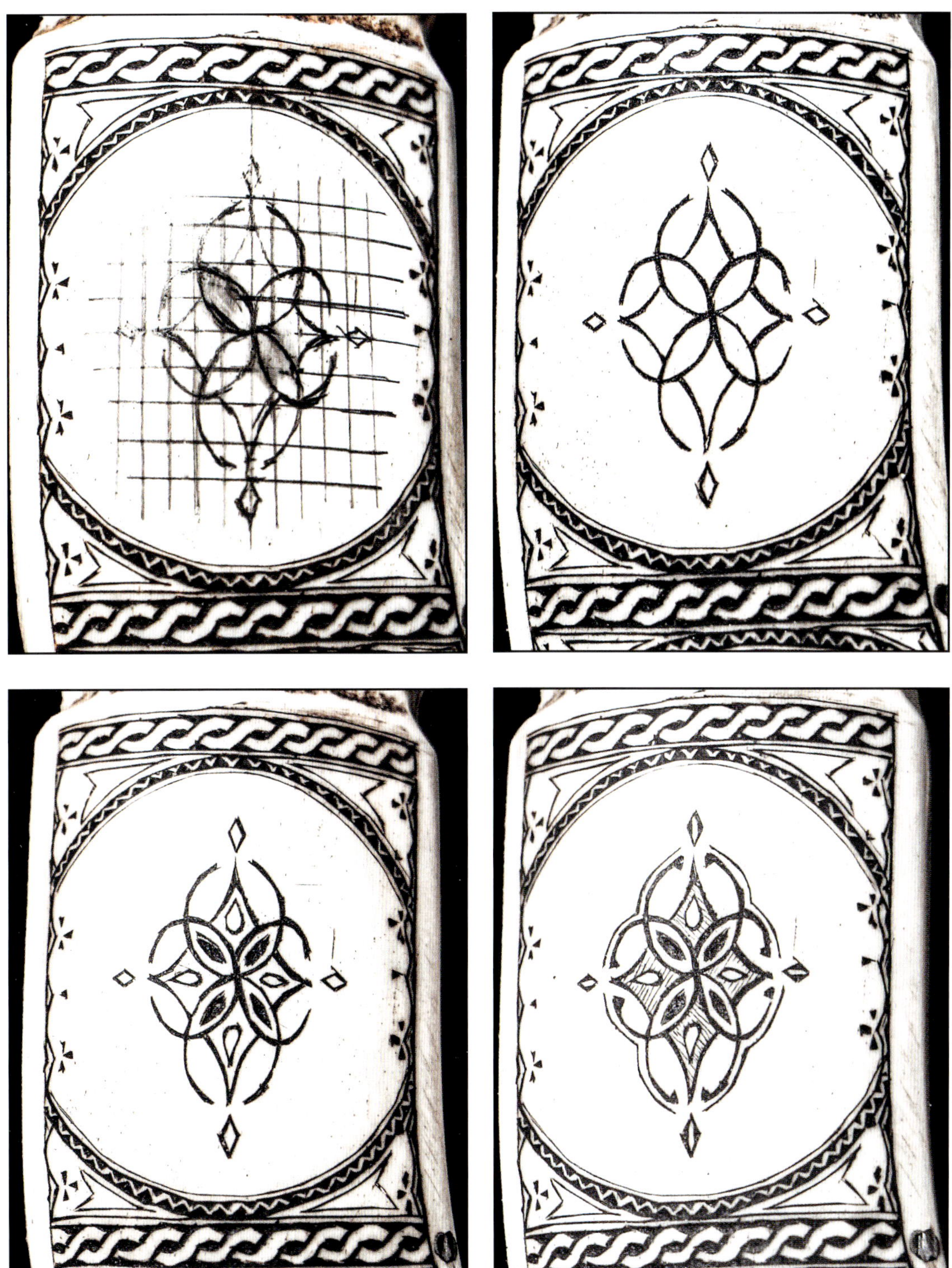

135–136–137–138 –To make this design I first draw a grid of 5/64-inch (2 mm) squares as a guide for the pattern.

1) Begin with the base lines of the pattern.

2) Color the lines you have cut with water and cacao. Don't apply oil-based color at this stage because it will be hard to sketch on the antler's surface with a pen. The grid is wiped away, and you will now use the cut lines as guides.

Belt Loop

For safety and performance the belt loop should be made of 3 braided leather strips. It should be one solid piece in one end and be joined together on the other to avoid tangling. Each strip should have the smooth side facing outwards when being twisted

Surface Finish

All scratches from sanding should be removed.

The handle should be polished with oil; it should never be varnished.

The Kosa

"Coffee, sipped from your own hand-made Kosa, definitely tastes better"

The Kosa

There is no exact English word for this very particular wooden cup which we call a Kosa. You may find different spellings which reflect slightly different pronunciations in Scandinavia. Where I live in the north of Sweden it has always been referred to as a Kosa so I will continue to use this term.

The Kosa is made from a burl which is a hard protuberance found on a number of different species of trees. I normally use birch since it is a hard and dense wood. The burls on birch trees usually have the shape of a half sphere.

When I'm hunting, fishing or simply out in the woods for a hike it's a great pleasure to use my old and worn coffee-soaked Kosa, which is now more or less black inside from use. Relaxing in front of the campfire I sometimes reminisce about where I found the wood for my Kosa and how I made it. This really adds value to your cup. Coffee, sipped from your own hand-made Kosa definitely tastes better.

There can be some disappointing setbacks related to making your Kosa. The most frequent one is discovering, after all the work you've done cutting a burl from a tree and beginning the first steps at home, that there is a small rotten part in the burl, often a "bark inclusion" aka "included bark", which makes it impossible to carve out the exact shape you had in mind for it.

139 – It is hard to say where you can most easily find a burl. This one was found in an old mixed forest with birch and pine in northern Sweden. Burls can be found on many types of trees and in various shapes and conditions. To be on the safe side it should have a minimum size of a honey-dew melon. You can manage with a slightly smaller size but only if the surface is smooth, so you don't have to remove much wood.

Permission

Sawing or chopping off a burl from a tree creates a wound which can accelerate the aging of the tree, depending on the size of the burl you've removed. Therefore, it's important to have an agreement with the land/tree owner before you do this.

Season

The winter is the best season to cut off a burl. At this time of year the least amount of sap is running through the tree. This lessens the possibility of the wood forming cracks as the burl dries. It's also easier to remove the burl from the trunk when it's cold, and there is less damage to the tree itself.

140 – You will need an axe and a chain saw. Remove two wedge-shaped pieces both above and below the protuberance. The top cut is shown in the bottom photo. Begin by making two 4-inch (10 cm) deep, right-angle cuts, approximately 8-inches (20 cm) above and below the burl. The tip of the wedge faces downwards on the cut below the burl. Finish cutting the wedges and remove them. The handle of the Kosa will almost always be the part of the burl facing upwards on the tree.

141 – With your axe make a cut through the bark on the left and right sides of the burl. Now, working from above, inside the area you cut out, use wedges and your axe to separate the burl from the trunk.

142 – Remove a thin layer from the outside of the burl to determine if there are any bark inclusions in the area from which the Kosa will be made. Your goal should be to follow the natural bend of the cup's handle to avoid torn grain. This burl had a bark inclusion that limited the possibility of making a larger handle.

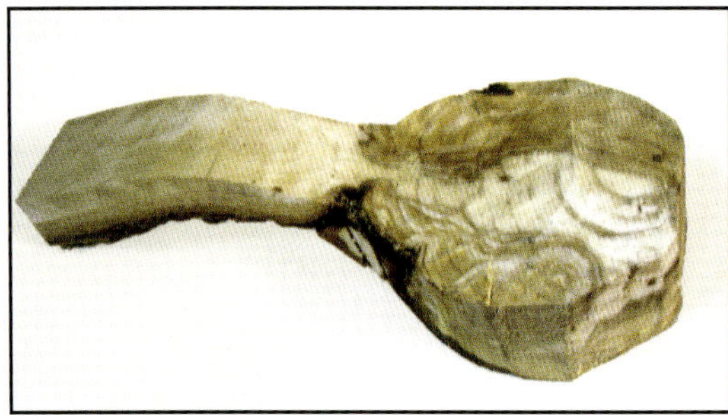

143 and **144** – As shown in the picture there is a lighter colored part of the wood which, in this case, is esthetically a good spot to begin the handle.

145 – A bark inclusion on the underside might be a determining factor in how the handle will be shaped. Hopefully, if you find an inclusion, it will only be in the surface layer of the wood.

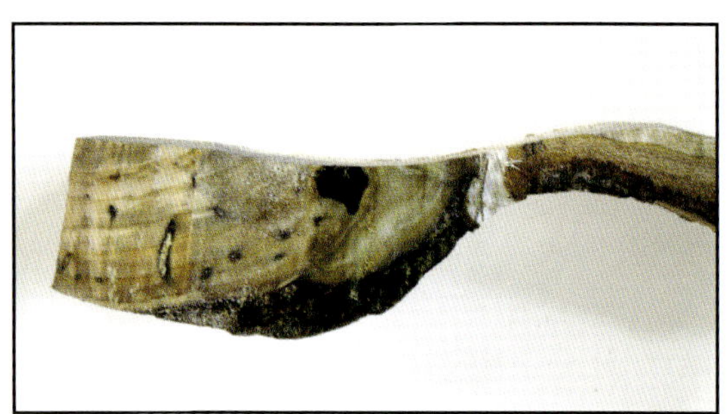

146 – Make a sketch of the shape of the Kosa as seen from above, fold it in half lengthwise (as shown in photo), then cut out the template.

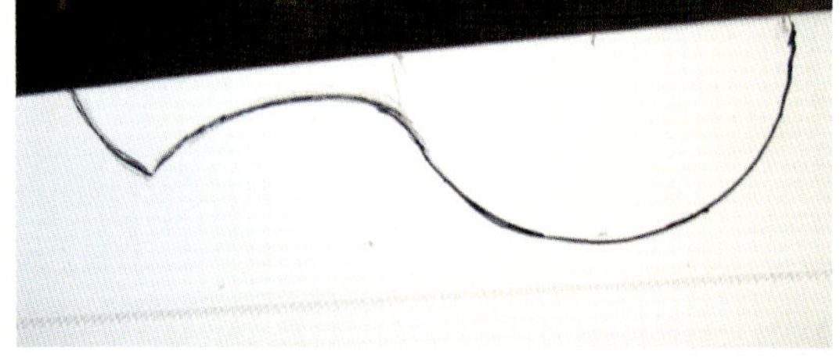

147 – Place the pattern on the burl. Try to place the narrowest part of the handle in your pattern on the narrowest part of the burl to optimize the thickness of the handle.

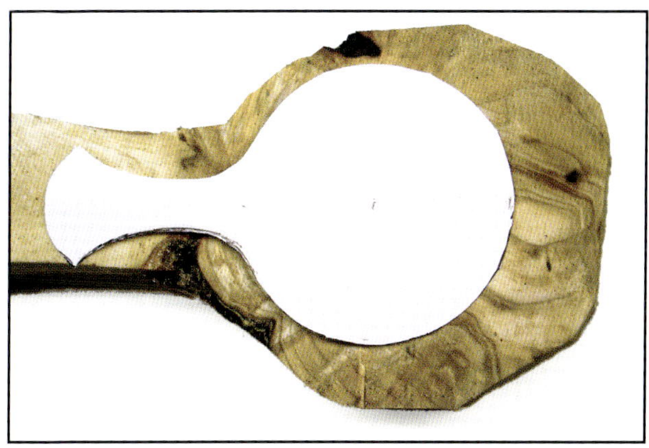

148 – Put a drill stop on an 5/16-inch (8 mm) drill bit. The stop should be placed approximately 19/32-inch (15 mm) from the final depth of the Kosa's bowl. Be aware of the fact that while drilling, stop rings will sometimes loosen and slide causing the hole to be drilled too deep.

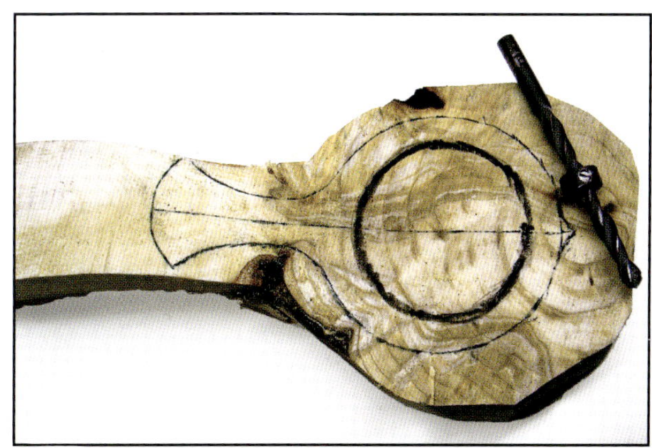

149 – Drill as many holes within the circle as possible. The more holes you make the easier your job will be in hollowing it out.

150 – Start to chip and dig-out as much wood as possible with a U-shaped wood chisel.

151 – I use a bent U-shaped wood chisel to level the bottom.

152 – The Kosa is carved following your sketched pattern, but leave some extra wood. Normally I leave an extra 1/2-inch (circa 12 mm). To prevent the wood from cracking apply a coat of wood glue to the outside of it (but NEVER to the inside of the bowl!).

153 – If you are working with fresh unseasoned wood, the Kosa must now be dried. There are many methods for doing this. My method at this stage is to put the roughly cut Kosa into wood shavings in a dark space. The drying time, depending on the thickness of the wood, is 11 to 12 months. To be safe, when working with a burl freshly cut from a tree, I make a note of when to start working on it again and keep it in the shavings for 1 year.

154 – The next step after drying the Kosa is to smooth out the inside of the bowl. Certain tools will make this process considerably easier. A ceramic ball burr is one such accessory.

155 – A round grinding point is another.

156 – When the initial smoothing work is completed on the inside of the bowl, an inflatable sanding ball is a great help in making it even smoother.

The following steps are for a Kosa that has been properly dried:

157 – The inside of the Kosa is now almost complete. It will be gently sanded later.

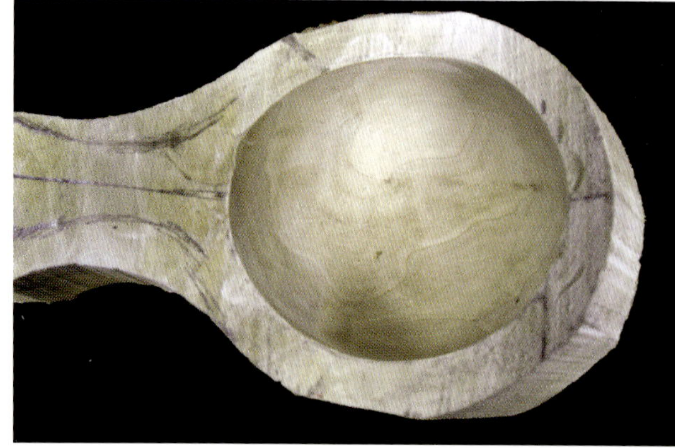

158 – The shape you want for the outside part of the Kosa (shown from the side in the photo) is first drawn and then roughly carved out. Normally I make a small flat surface on the bottom of the cup to facilitate standing the Kosa on a table. The exact placement of this flat spot needs to be checked now and then since hand-made Kosas have a tendency to be heavier in the handle, particularly after the parts made of antler are attached.

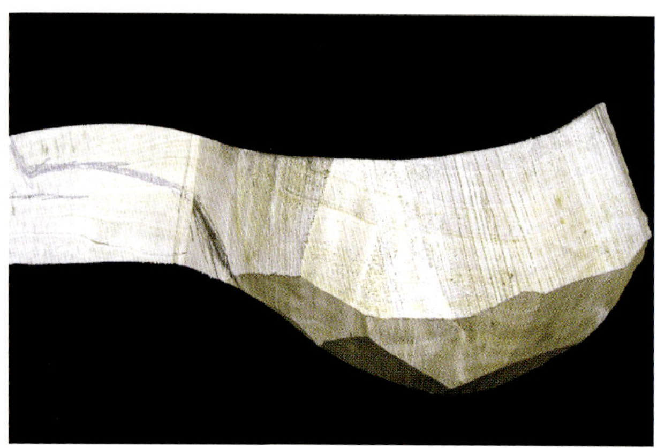

159 – Roughly finish the entire Kosa bowl area, both on the inside and the outside.

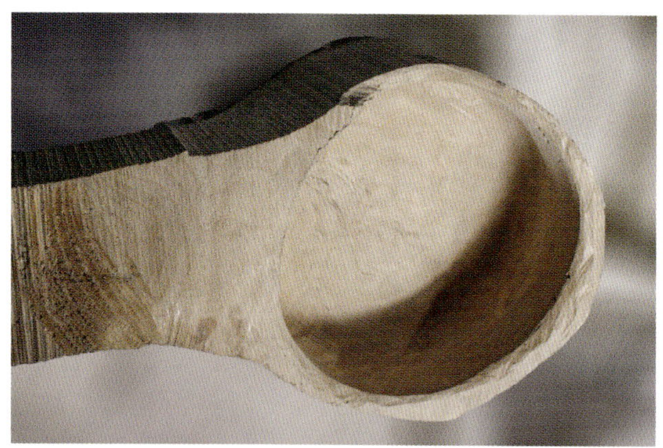

160 – Sketch the shape of the handle on a stiff piece of paper and cut out the template.

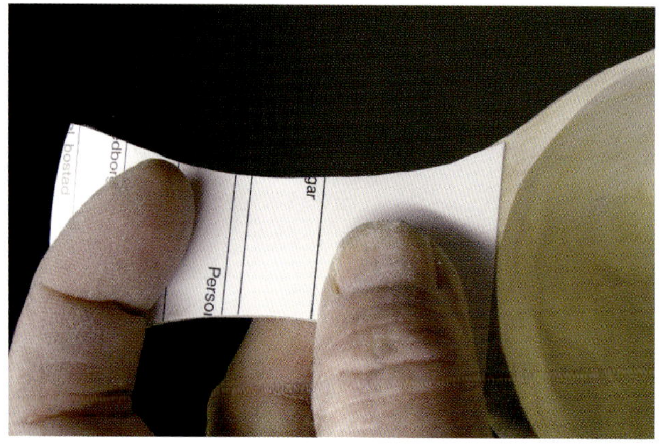

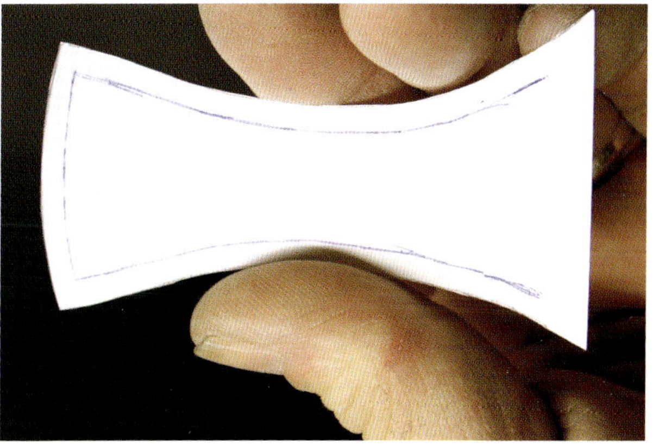

161 - Sketch a line 3/16-inch (4-5 mm) inside the outer edge of the template. Antler inlay, to be shown successively, will be placed in the area defined by those lines. The part of the sketch—not yet completed in the photo—facing the bowl part of the Kosa should follow the curve of the edge of the hole at a distance of 3/16-inch (4-5 mm) from the hollowed-out part (photo 164).

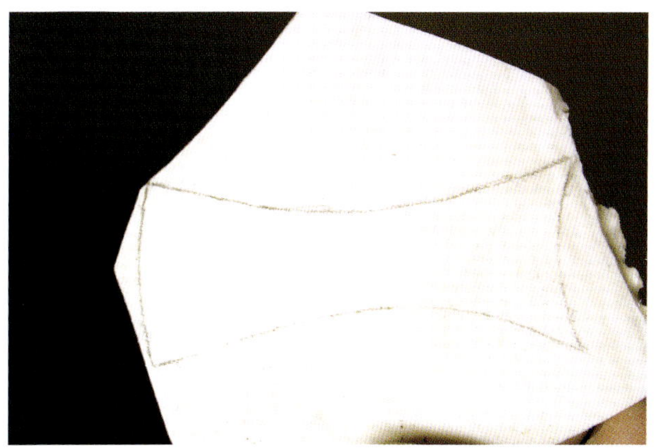

162 - Sketch the inlay design from the template onto a piece of 3/64-inch to 5/64-inch (1-2 mm) thick antler. In this case the antler is from a moose.

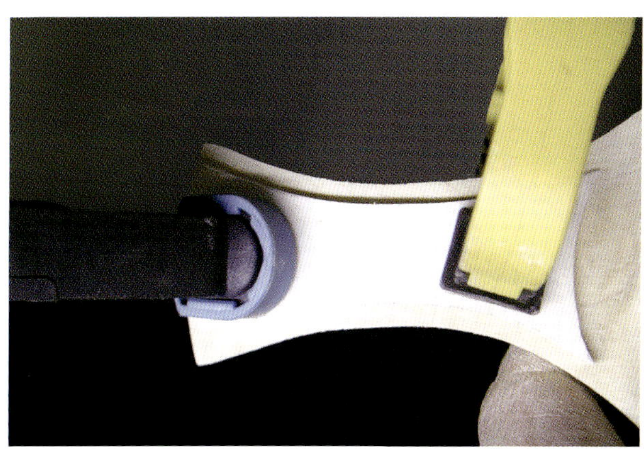

163 - Clamp the piece of antler onto the handle and trace its outline onto the handle.

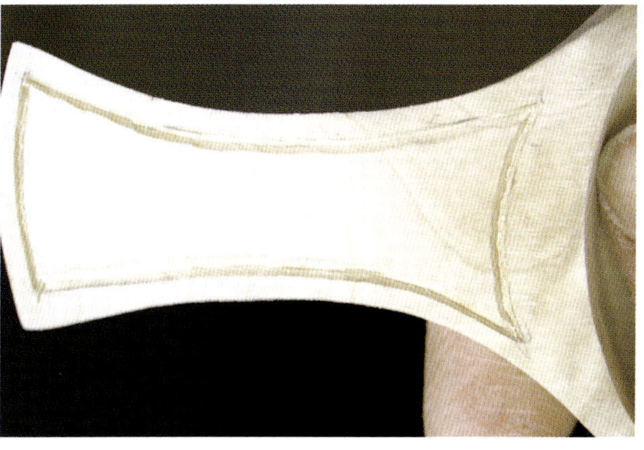

164 - The wood within the area for the inlay must be removed to a depth of 1/16-inch (1.5 mm). Begin by cutting along the traced line at a right angle to the surface.

165 – The wood is removed with a sharp chisel and/or a grinding bit.

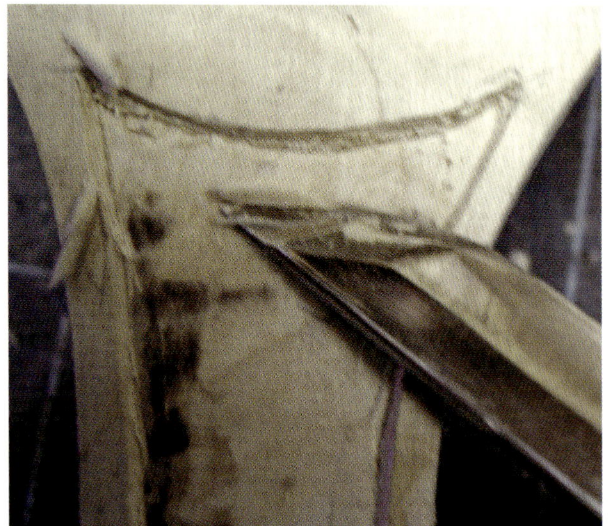

166 – When the piece of antler fits perfectly into the carved-out section I then glue it in with a strong epoxy glue.

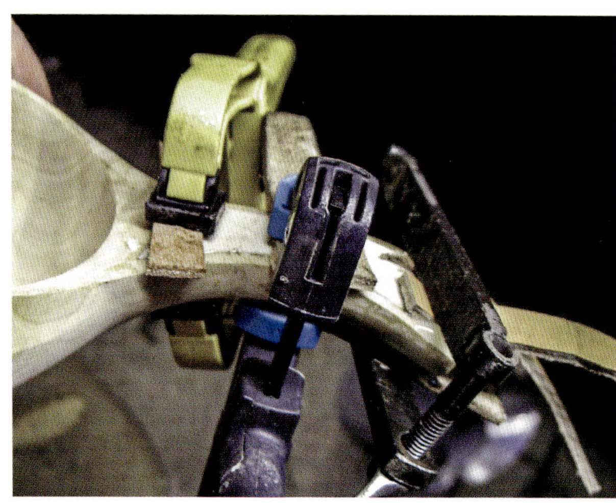

Alternative Handle

Alternatively, the antler plate can be attached directly to the surface of the handle.

167 – Erase or ignore the sketch of the line inside the outer edge of the template used for the inlaid handle. This is because the antler plate in this process will be as wide as the handle. The part of the template facing the bowl of the Kosa should be straight and at a distance of 3/16-inch to 3/8-inch (5-10 mm) from the beginning of the hollowed-out edge of the bowl.

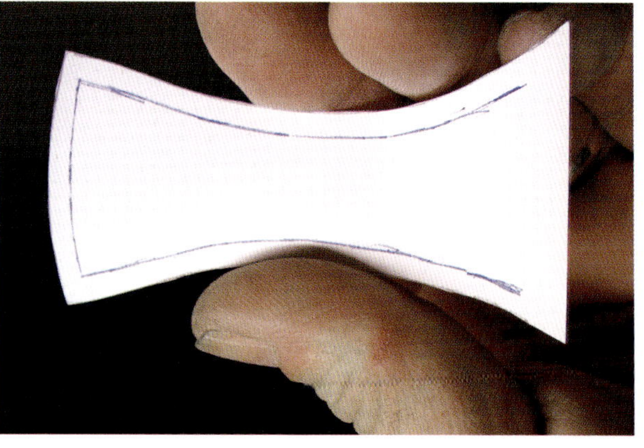

168 – Along the straight line of the template which faces the bowl (approximately 3/8-inch (10 mm) from the edge of the hole) make a 1/16-inch (2 mm) deep cut in the handle at a right angle to the surface of the handle. Use a saw with an extra-thin blade such as a Japanese saw. Now carve an even and flat slope from a position 5/64 to 1/8-inch (2-3 cm) above the cut (i.e., from the direction of the handle's end), down to the bottom of the 5/64-inch (2 mm) cut.

169 – Use the saw again and place it flat along the carved slope. Make a 1/16-inch (1.5 mm) deep cut towards the opening of the Kosa's bowl. The resulting cut or lip will be used to anchor the antler in the handle.

170 – Bevel the antler at the bottom in order to be able to wedge it into the cut.

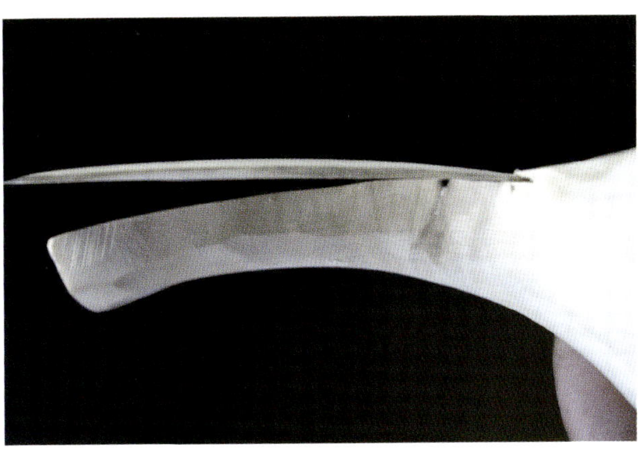

171 – Put the plate in place and bend it along the handle to see if it fits tightly. The antler should be easy to bend if it wasn't "burnt" (dried out) when sanding it thin.

172 – The plate is now removed, glued with a strong epoxy, inserted again into the cut and clamped down using several clamps, with one attached very close to, or over, the cut as shown in the photo.

173 – When the glue has hardened, work on the plate making it is the same shape as the handle. The plate should be "riveted" as an extra precaution. I use a 5/64-inch (2 mm) screw. I put a fast setting super glue in the screw hole before putting in the screw. The Kosa is now to be sanded (see the section on surface treatment).

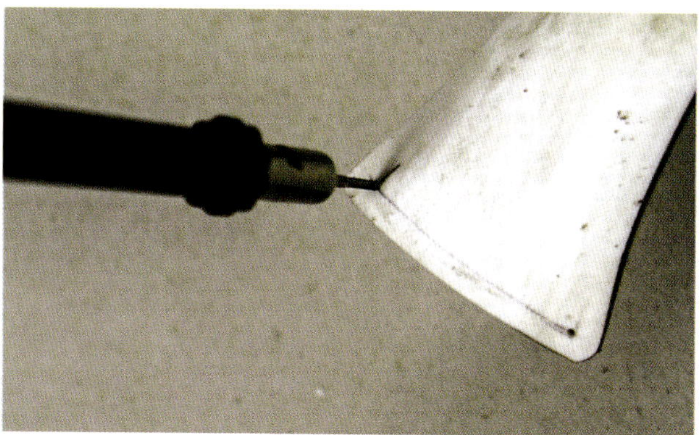

Patterning

Patterning of a Kosa doesn't differ from the procedure used on an Antler Knife. More information is to be found under the same heading in the Antler Knife section of this book. Nevertheless, to give you some extra information I will describe how it is done on this Kosa.

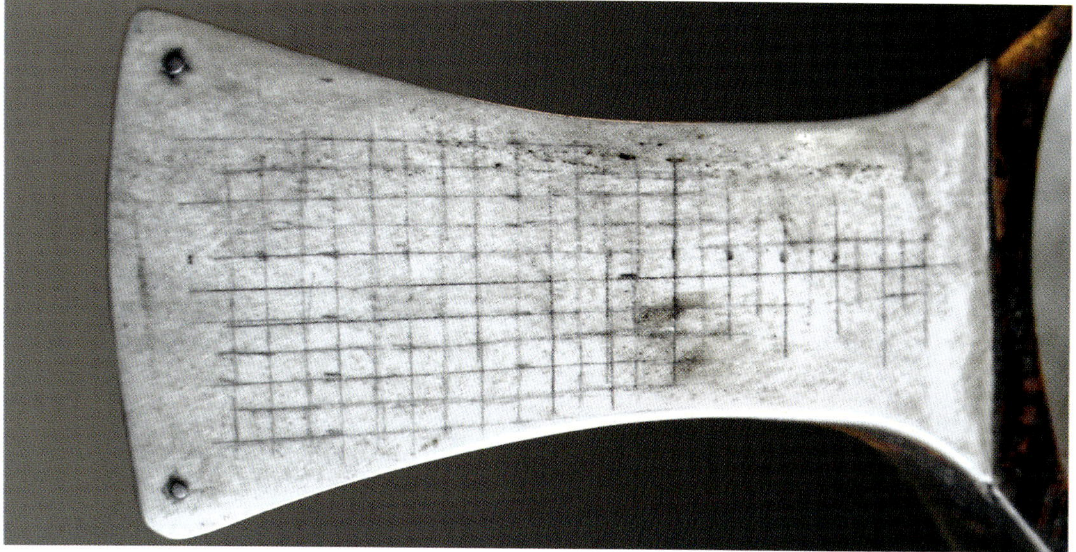

174 – Start the procedure using a sharp pencil and drawing a grid using 2 mm squares. The antler must not be polished before making the grid, since it would then be impossible to sketch on the glossy surface with your pencil.

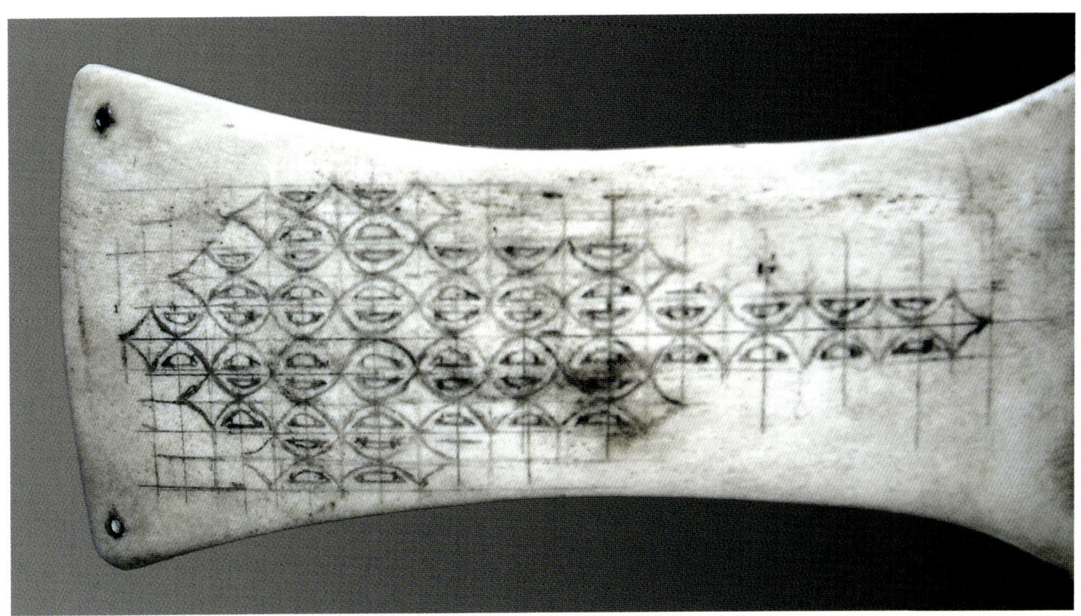

175 – There are different ways of sketching the pattern; some do it a bit at a time while others sketch the entire pattern immediately. I do something in between. I sketch quite a bit at first carefully building up the geometric pattern that I want. To prevent accidently rubbing off or smearing your pencil sketch with your hand you can spray a thin layer of art fixative or hair spray on the sketch to protect it.

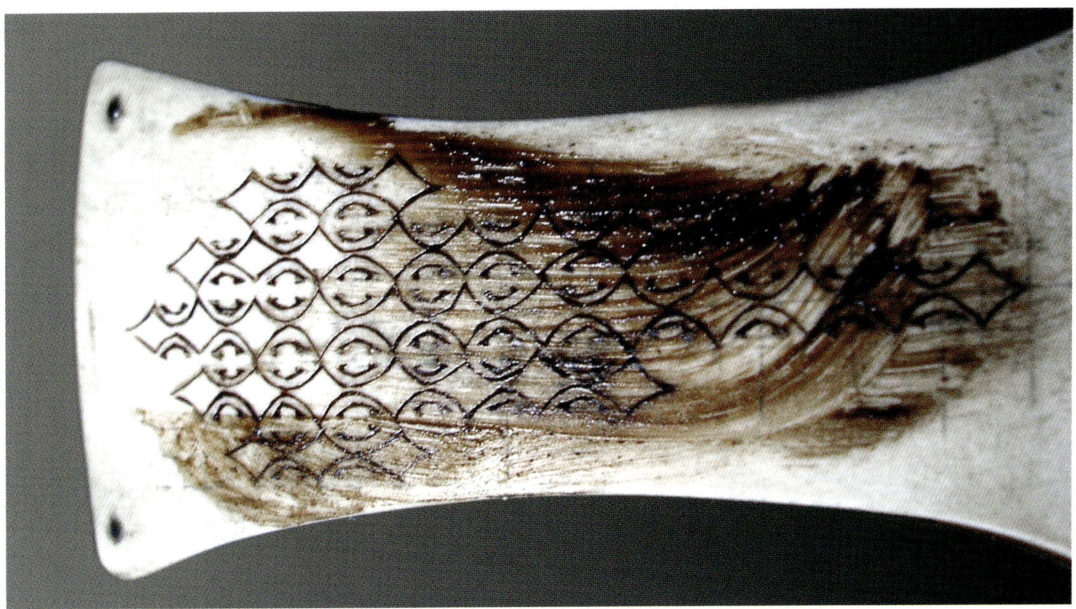

176 – The sketched pattern is cut along the pencil lines from two angles (making a V) with a very sharp knife or an engraving tool. The first stain is made with oil pigment. Excess oil on the antler is wiped off with your thumb or finger and not paper since that would absorb the stain. But you must remove any remaining oil from the unmarked surface, otherwise it will be difficult to sketch the rest of the pattern.

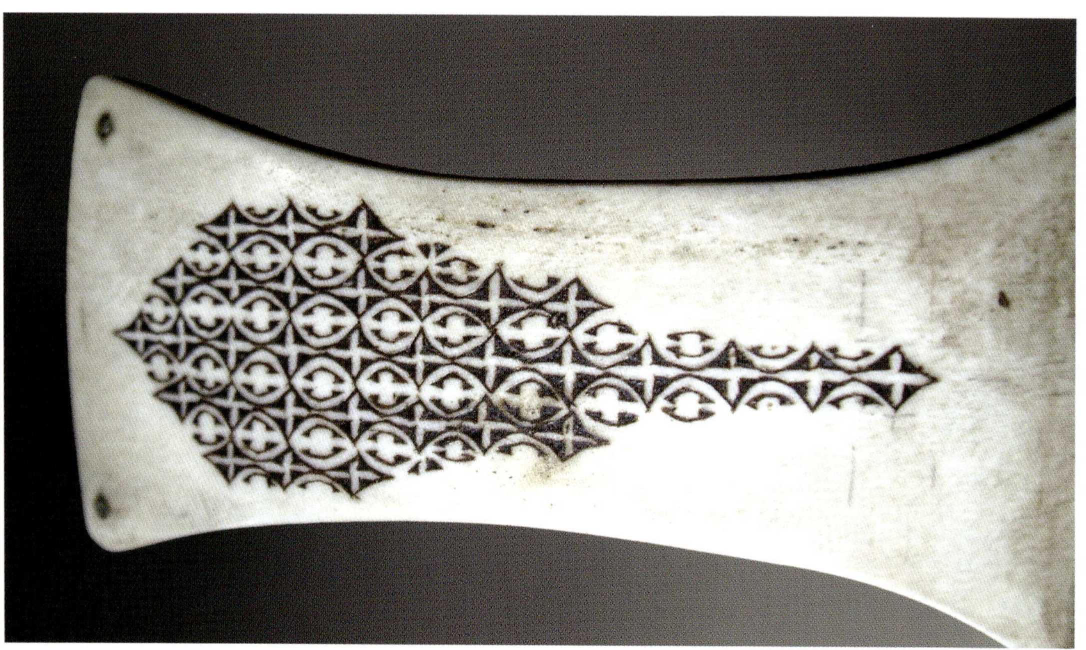

177 – Here is an example of how to build up and add to your pattern step-by-step. I have now added white crosses to the design.

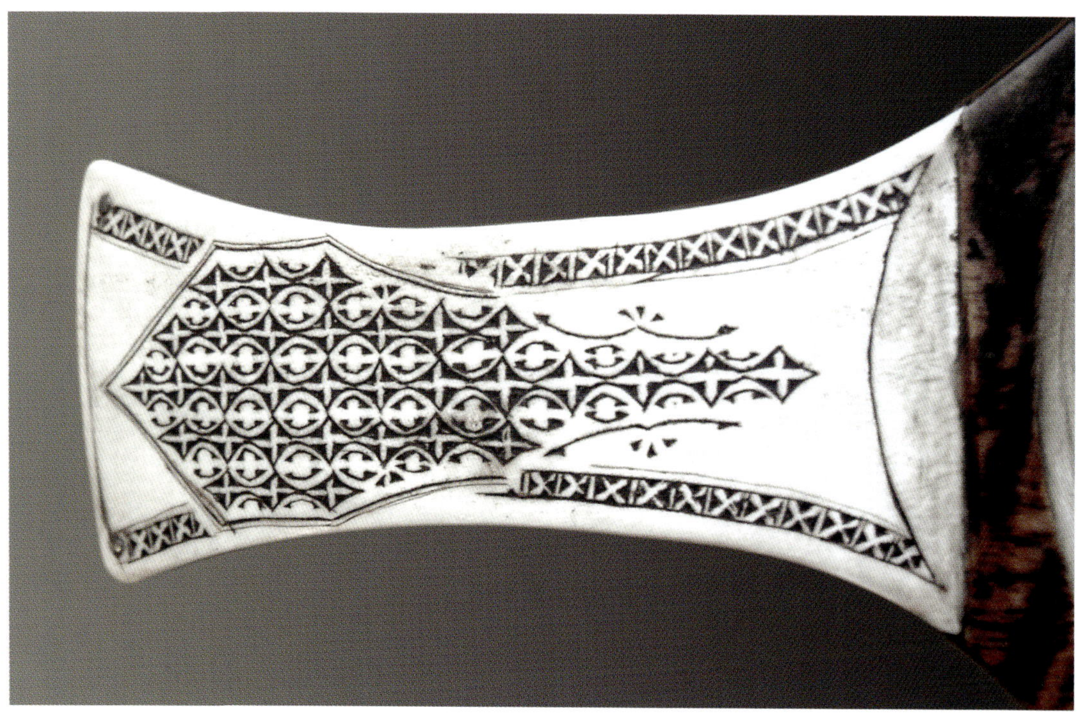

178 – The work continues by adding different patterns and staining. This is the final pattern.

Alternative Pattern

How to make a pattern with a "Rose" in the center.

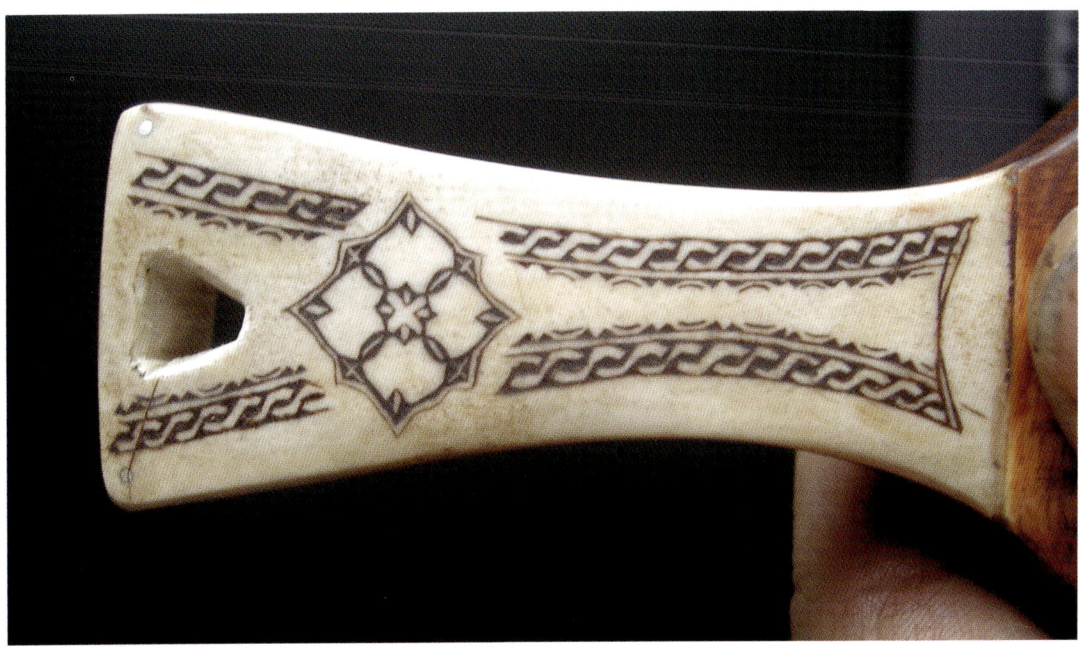

179 – This is the finished pattern. I will show how it was made.

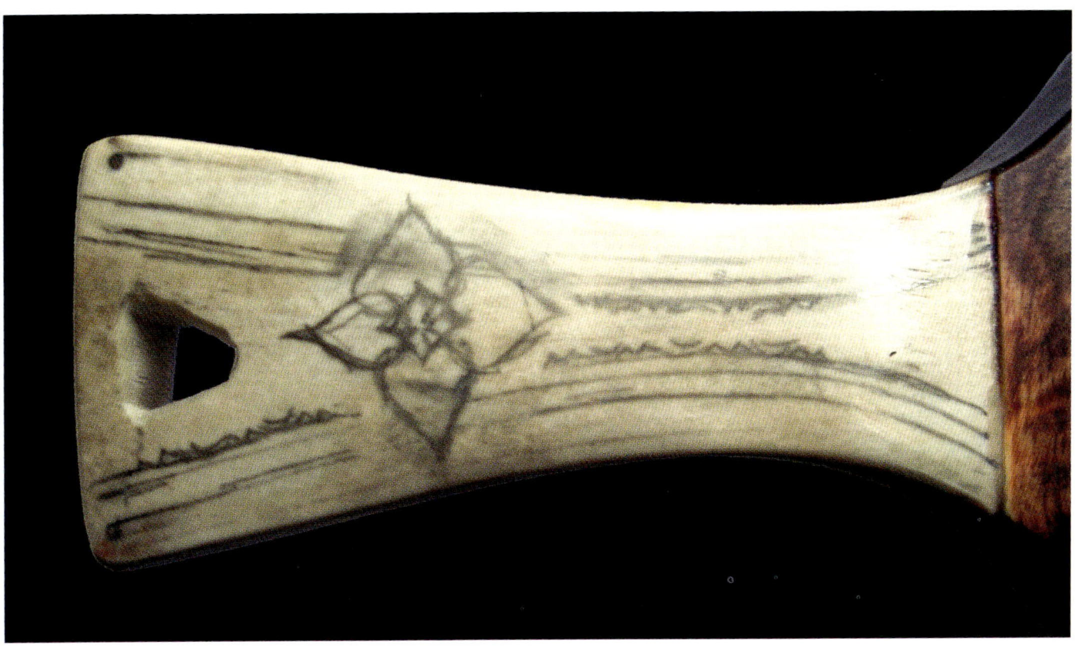

180 – Start by beginning to pencil a sketch on the handle and deciding how to build up the pattern making sure that the dimensions of your projected design and its placement will fit in the given space.

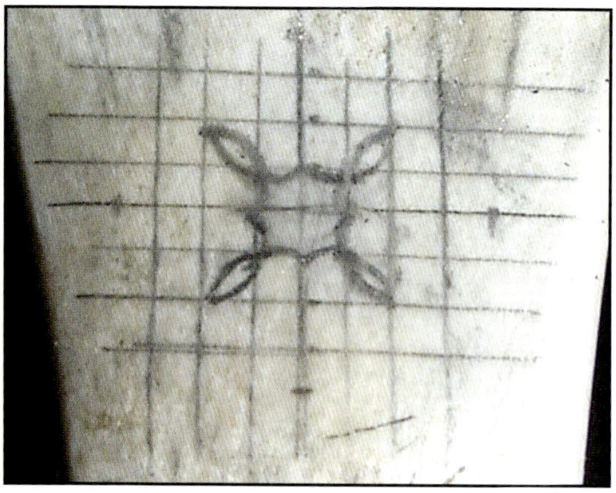

181 and 182 – For the Rose begin by making a grid with 5/64-inch (2 mm) squares. Then start with the center of the Rose.

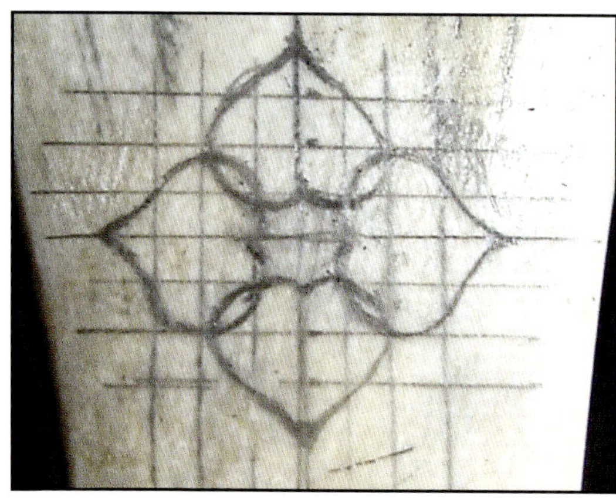

183 – After the basic pattern is cut the first stain is applied. As previously mentioned, you must remove any excess stain from the surface to allow you to sketch the rest of the pattern.

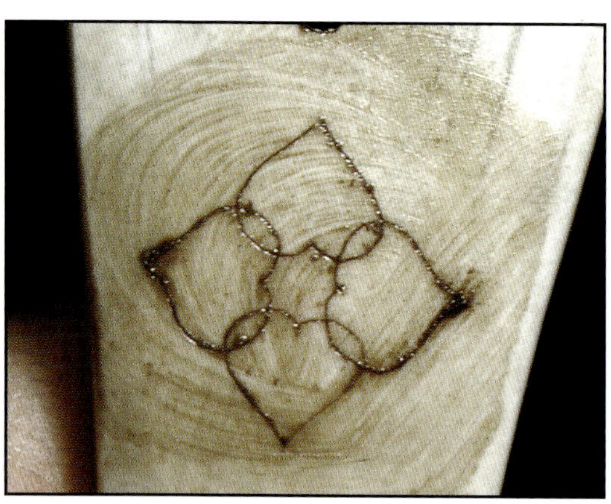

184 – The excess stain on the antler is removed with your thumb or finger and not paper which would absorb all the stain.

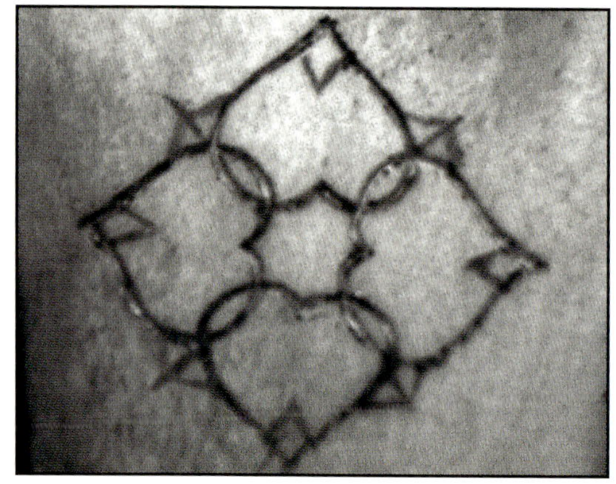

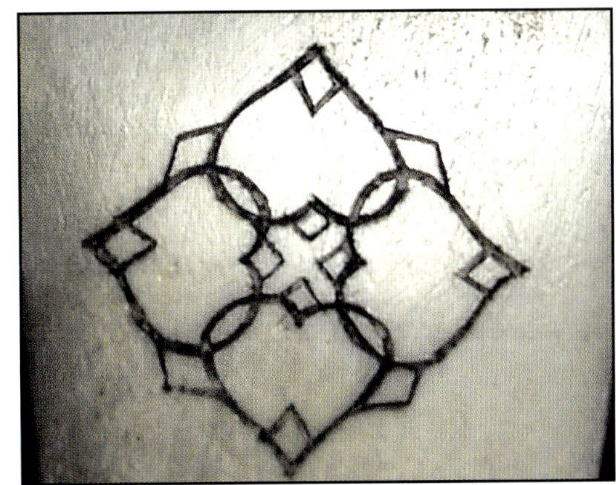

185 – The pattern is built up step-by-step.

186 – A shadow effect is now given by cutting new lines next to the ones where stain has already been applied. I normally carve these lines without having sketched them. I simply try to keep them at the same distance from the stained lines.

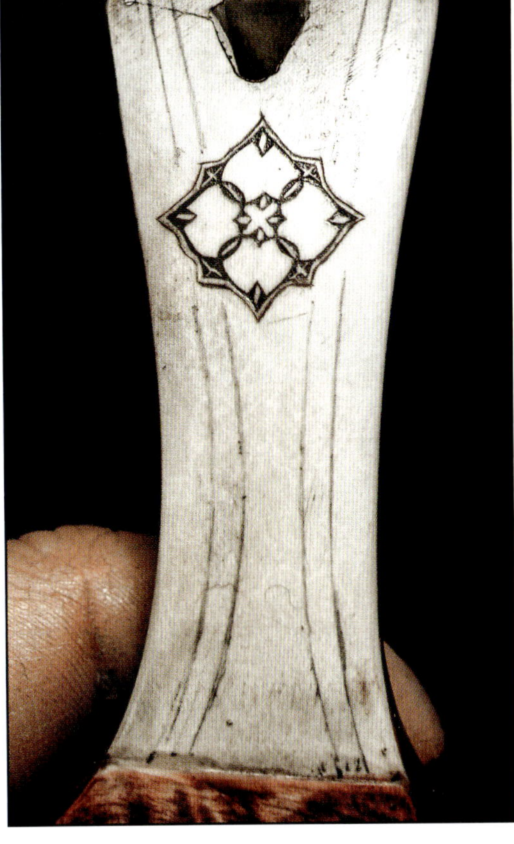

187 – The Rose is completed. The next step is to make borders along the handle which are interrupted by the Rose design.

Ulf Avander

Ulf Avander has been working with antler as a material for knife handles, knife sheaths and other antler craft for more than 50 years. Over this long period he has learned both from the old masters and also from his contemporaries and has developed his own style.

Ulf lives with his wife in northern Sweden, where he enjoys creating antler knives, kosas, and other antler craft. He's an avid sportsman who loves Sweden's great outdoors and is often away fishing, hunting and hiking.

To see Ulf's newest knives, sheaths and kosas visit his site:

www.UlfaAB.se

FORGED:
Making a Knife with Traditional Blacksmith Skills

"Concise and simplified instructions along with the illustrations made for an informative and easy to follow plan. The injection of tips kept me wanting to read and learn more. The simple, yet effective layout of information and instruction made this an enjoyable read. A great source of tips and tricks for any bladesmith from start to finish. This book is a must read for up-and-coming bladesmiths. It inspired me to try my hand at an all-traditional knife build in the future." – **Lee Crawford, Professional knifemaker and winner of the Naval competition in TV's "Forged in Fire" in the tournament of the Military Branches, Central States Metal Artisans Newsletter.**

".... does an excellent job explaining the process of forging a knife but also in instilling enthusiasm for doing this the traditional way." – **The Forum, newsletter of The Guild of Metalsmiths**

"Lavishly illustrated, and with technique very clearly explained, this book is a WINNER. Highly recommended if you want a NO-BS primer on how to forge a blade. Beautifully photographed, a very pleasant surprise." – **Stuart Geisler, Moderator, The Original International Blacksmithing group Facebook page**

This book will teach you to hand build a knife using the traditional method of blacksmiths of old — FORGING.
Traditional forging of a knife blade is a process which uses the ancient techniques of moving hot steel with hammer and anvil alone into a knife-form that is ready for filing, heat treating and sharpening with no or very minimal electric grinding. This book also teaches traditional fit-and-finish skills using only hand tools. It explains an ancient riveted full-tang handle construction system that surpasses modern methods.

"In my early blacksmithing years, I was lucky to get to know some old smiths who wrangled hot iron every day just to make a living. They unselfishly taught me traditional blacksmithing skills and knife forging methods. Every time I use those skills and methods, I honor their friendships, and by teaching you, the reader, we keep alive the memory of those old-time iron pounders." - **Paul White**

The Blacksmith's Project Book: Intermediate & Advanced Projects from European Masters

"This book would be helpful for any blacksmith trying to broaden their ideas and technique." - **Monica Coyne, Artist Blacksmith**

"... an exceptional publication." - **Northern Rockies Blacksmiths Association Newsletter**.

"Fills a void in blacksmithing texts available today ... a serious treatment of a large collection of different skills ... priced slightly below what comparable advanced text books are selling for. With the wealth of information contained it is truly a bargain." - **Bob Menard, The New England Blacksmiths Newsletter.**

"This is an exceptional book with many projects that I plan to attempt myself." - **Barry Myers, On the Anvil Newsletter (The Phillip Simmons Artist Blacksmith Guild).**

"... sparks the imagination, informs and inspires." - **Amy Mook, Hot Iron News, (Northwest Blacksmith Association).**

"The pieces presented in this book have motivated me to continue to attempt to expand my skills and their use in the creation of art in metal." - **Jeff Jarrett, The Appalachian Area Chapter of Blacksmiths Newsletter.**

Clearly explains the necessary steps and techniques for completing projects which include metallic fusion, damascening, chromatic finishing techniques, fold-forming, patination, sculpture forging, and other interesting topics.

Hardcover, 248 pages, over 900 color phots, 9.5-inches x 11.25-inches.

Secrets of the Forge: Beginning & Intermediate Projects for Blacksmiths

"There is a wealth of knowledge in this excellent book. Exceptionally well organized and presented, "Secrets of the Forge" is unreservedly recommended for personal, professional, community, and technical college library collections on the art and science of blacksmithing". **- Paul T. Vogel, the Midwest Book Review**

In this fascinating and useful project book 24 Italian master blacksmiths share their techniques with you on a great variety of jobs, ranging from the basic and simple to the more complex and artistic.

The individual steps of each job are clearly illustrated with high quality close-up color photos. The text in this new translation has been expertly edited so all technical details are clear to the reader. The book begins with basic jobs such as twisting bars and making spearhead shapes and scrolls. As you progress the projects become more complex and involve forging truly artistic iron sculptures such as a duck in flight, a snail, flowers, a dragon, a nude, and more.

The book concludes with two highly specialized projects: making a Damascus steel blade, and the construction of a fully functional hand-forged lock. There is a wealth of knowledge in this excellent book. Experienced professional smiths will get as much from it as novices. Antonello Rizzo is also the author of *The Blacksmith's Project Book: Intermediate & Advanced Projects from European Masters* which picks up where *Secrets of the Forge* leaves off.